RED SOILS OF TSAVO

*I am deeply grateful to Elaine, Dilshad and Shakil
for helping me with the preparation of this work.
Without Gula's encouragement this book would
never have been in print. I also wish to thank
Mr. R Ramaer for allowing me to use the picture
Of the steam locomotive on the front piece.
For the benefit of steam enthusiasts it is Class EC 3
4-8-4 + 4-8-4 No. 5813*

RED SOILS OF TSAVO

M G VISRAM

First published by M G Visram in 1987 as *On a Plantation in Kenya'*
in Mombasa , Kenya

This Edition published by **Q Hunter Ltd**. P.O. Box 81403
Mombasa, Kenya.   **e-mail address:**
                         tsavo.hunterq@yahoo.co.uk

Printing History

Reprinted	1988
Reprinted	**1989**
Reprinted	**1991**
Reprinted	**1992**
Reprinted	**1995**
Reprinted	**1998**
Reprinted	**2007**

**Available in UK
at amazon.co.uk**

Visram, M.G

Red soils of
Tsavo / by M.G.
Visram

967.
62

1855473

Printed by Rodwell Press Ltd. P.O. Box 90252, Mombasa, Kenya

In loving memory of
my father

By the same author

ALLIDINA VISRAM
THE TRAIL BLAZER

BEYOND THE BAOBAB TREE

PREFACE

All this happened a long time ago. The events are set in Kenya at the stage when the end of the colonial rule was looming on the horizon. Those were the days when Nairobi was *in fact* a city in the sun, all neat and clean. In all corners of the city one would see bougainvilleas in their multitude of hues, no matter what time of the year it was. Come November and Jacaranda trees would come out in full bloom, as if trying to outdo the bougainvilleas. Driving down from Nairobi to the coastal town of Mombasa was fun. One did not have to worry about unpredictably driven trucks and minibuses. Insecurity was unheard of. As long as you did not run into a herd of elephants crossing the road, (common in those days), you were fine. Even travelling by train from Uganda to Kenya, was an experience that for some, can be a lifetime memory. Having left Kampala in Uganda the previous day, one would wake up in the morning to see a Garratt Steam locomotive serpentining the train from the Highlands of western Kenya into the Rift Valley. Leaning out of the window, one would be hit in the face by high altitude's early morning crispy cold wind. This would be mingled with the aroma of the early morning fresh coffee that the waiters would be serving in different compartments. Stations with names like *Timboroa, Equator, Plateau,* some as high as 9000 feet above sea level, would glide by in the early morning mist. Everything seemed so surreal! Then, having sunk into the bottom of the Rift Valley, the train would make a straight run across its basin, as the majestic Mount Longonot remained in sight for the better part of this section of the journey. At the other end of the Valley, the steam engine, with thick black smoke belching out of its chimney, would give all its might to pull the train out of it over the Kijabe escarpment. Finally, in the evening it would push along the stretch that is now Uhuru Highway and ease into Nairobi Railway Station. During the two-hour stopover at Nairobi, a fresh locomotive would replace the tired one that would then pull the train and disappear enthusiastically into the night on its final stage of the journey to the coast. Voi, then a remote spot in southeastern Kenya, was the only designated stopover during this final lap. Only those who loved this ride would understand Mark Twain's deep-rooted nostalgia for paddleboats of Mississippi River.

This was also the time when a handful of us, through divine design or call it luck, had our lives intertwined at a sisal estate at Voi. (Sisal is a tropical plant resembling a pineapple top, but much larger in dimension, reaching about four to five feet in height. Its leaves are crushed in a special machine called decorticator and yields fiber which is used to make ropes and twines). In retrospect, I feel that we were all a touch high on eccentricity.

It all started in 1957. My elder brother Rustam and I gave up schooling in Uganda and came to look after this sisal plantation our father had bought some ten years back. I was in my teens. This plantation was adjoining the recently created Tsavo National Park. We shared a common boundary with the park and had more than our fair share of problems with the wild game. Operating a sisal estate is a very extensive exercise. It needs a diverse range of staff: carpenters, mechanics, field assistants, accountants etc. In an exceptional case like ours, it even requires a hunter to keep the big game at bay, not allowing them to eat away the sisal plants. Designation of a particular staff also reflects in his personality. A hunter may not think twice about going to the field in the middle of the night and bringing down an elephant or two, while a clerk would avoid going to the outdoor toilet after dusk, even at the risk of bursting his bladder! There was one particular foreign visitor who came regularly once a year during the full moon and took pot shots at the moon for an hour or so with his .375 rifle. We all would sit in a semicircle behind him at a respectable distance, trying to figure out what was driving him to such insanity. Before going to sleep in his tent he would spit on the ground and say angrily. "The damn thing got away again." We had to endure them and some of them had to tolerate us.

The following pages contain some of the events that took place on the plantation. I say 'some events' because others had either racial, tribal or religious connotations. I feel these undertones are best left alone. Again some incidents were of too personal a nature to include in this type of work.

On a few occasions I have mentioned steam locomotives of Eastern Africa. Sadly they are no longer there. Some have been preserved at the Railway Museum in Nairobi, each of them looking like embalmed remains of some magnanimous personality: Very quiet and totally lifeless. Future generations will never see those roaring and thundering machines in action again. But then, the old – however much you loved it – has to make way for the new. Life is meant to be that way.

M G V

IN THE BEGINNING

Many years ago you asked me a question: *'Do you still remember what it was like at Voi in those days?'*

I looked at you absent-mindedly. At that particular moment my mind was preoccupied with petty problems and thoughts. I went on biting my nails and your question remained unanswered.

Recently our car had a breakdown at Bachuma railway station. It was nothing major, just a broken fan belt. Someone volunteered to go to look for a replacement. I was not sure what to do until the car was repaired. Without any special reason I walked up to the railway station and leisurely strolled up and down the line. It was about five in the evening. There was not a soul in sight. The stationmaster or his assistant might have been tapping over the morse code machine or doing whatever was required of them to give free passage to an occasional train that passed that point. This is not a railway station in the strict sense. Places like these serve mostly as crossing points for the single track line we have in Kenya. One of the trains travelling in the opposite direction is made to wait on the side line while the other passes through.

Momentarily I stopped walking to watch the Taita Hills in the west. A little later my attention was drawn to the railway line itself. The two shiny bars of metal became narrower and narrower as they disappeared into the plains. The scene

1

was breathtaking. But for a broken fan belt I would have missed this moment of Africa's magic dripping into the system to a point where one is addicted: the vastness of the land; fresh and clean air; simplicity and innocence of a peasant's mind, and clear blue and wide sky . . . All these things are rubbed into one subconsciously.

For reasons best known only to the force that governs the function of a mind, I remembered the question you had asked. 'What was it like at Voi in those days?' I sat down on a concrete culvert as thoughts and events of those bygone days began to link up.

Since you yourself have lived in Kenya in the past you must have seen a baobab tree. What I strongly doubt is if you have paid any special attention to this tree.

The baobab tree is a strange creation of nature. It differs from all other trees in practically every respect. Its unusually fat trunk is topped by crooked branches. These branches are bereft of leaves except for a few weeks in a year. The baobab is also a shy tree. It prefers to be apart from another baobab. There is something sad about this tree. Altogether it portrays an image of an old maid who has over-waited for her Prince Charming to come and sweep her off her feet.

There was one such baobab tree next to the railway line about two miles east of Voi. At that point the railway track, having had a straight run of forty miles over Taru Desert, gradually turned left and sank into a basin surrounded by hills. That is where Voi railway station was.

It is still there . . .

It was at this point that late one cold and windy evening many years ago two men in their coupe compartment of the passenger train looked at a cluster of lights in the distance.

'That must be our station,' observed one of them.

The other simply kept staring out of the window without saying anything.

They had boarded the 'One-up' – the overnight train

from Mombasa to Nairobi as it was referred to in those days – some four hours earlier. For the better part of the journey they had talked very little and smoked incessantly. The elder of the two wore a felt hat. It was reputed that he had never removed his felt hat. Only a person very intimate with him would have known if he went to sleep with his hat on or not. The other man wore a white topee.

They were business partners. They had met accidentally and started a small sawmill in Uganda in the first year of the Second World War. Going was tough. Spares for running their mill were difficult to come by due to war shortages. But they had the knack of getting things done. Between the two of them they became saw doctors, steam engine tube cleaners, turners, fitters or whatever was required of them. Timber was in short supply. Whatever they produced was sold – at a good price too. Working in forests, miles from nowhere and at the most odd hours, they prospered. By the time the war was over they had a chain of six sawmills and a small but efficient team of workers. They also had a credit in their bank of some sixty thousand pounds. The trip to Mombasa was to investigate whether they could diversify into any other venture. But there was nothing around Mombasa that interested them. However, someone in Mombasa had told them that at the foot of Mount Kilimanjaro in Tanganyika there was a German-owned sawmill for sale. It operated on electricity generated by turbines installed on one of the rivers gushing down from the great mountain. This interested them and they set off on their way to Tanganyika.

Voi was the junction for the Tanganyika line.

The train to Tanganyika was due to leave Voi the next afternoon and they would have to spend the night at the Dak Bungalow operated by the railway authorities. The Dak Bungalow turned out to be very neat and clean and was run by courteous staff. There were hardly any other guests. Food was delicious; beds were clean, starched, white sheets and

3

brown blanket with KUR (for Kenya Uganda Railway) very prominently inscribed over them lest someone should get too attached to them.

'Good morning gentlemen!' a man in a white suit and a black tie greeted them as soon as they settled down to breakfast the next morning. It was the chief steward. His name was Pinto, the partners were to learn later. 'I hope you slept well,' he added.

'It was not too bad,' answered the junior partner.

'What time does our train leave?' asked the senior partner.

'It leaves at two o'clock. You have the whole morning to look around Voi, if you wish,' Pinto replied.

'I wonder what there is to be seen in a God-forsaken place like this!' said one of them.

'There is a shopping center about half a mile down this road,' Pinto was pointing to the murram road that ran out of the station and disappeared into the thick Acacia bush. 'There are not many shops, maybe about six or seven. But one of the shopkeepers sells very good Australian cheese. He gets it from the military camp at Mackinnon Road. God only knows how he does it. But the cheese is really good.' The steward was eager to please his guests. Any imported item was a luxury during immediate post-war days.

The two people at the table were more interested in the fried eggs and marmalade in front of them than imported cheese being sold half a mile away. Mr. Pinto must have resented their indifference. How could sane men take no interest in such a scarce commodity! He paused for a while and then added:

'There is also a sisal factory down the road.' Pinto regretted saying this. He thought it was senseless talking to these indifferent people. To the likes of Pinto of the railway who lived uncomplicated and very simple

4

and routine lives, it was difficult to conceive that something you could not eat or drink could be of much significance.

'What is sisal?' asked one of his guests, even surprising Mr Pinto.

'There are plants that grow around,' he said, not quite sure himself now it came to it. 'These people cut their long leaves and feed them into a large crusher. On the other side of the crusher come some white strings – er no – not strings, but they call them fibres. It is said that you can make rope out of it! I am not entirely sure. You see, it is not really my line.'

The partners looked at each other across the table. Their minds worked in unison. They had six hours to spare. Why not walk down the murram road that led to the factory producing this novel thing. They wanted to know what sisal was.

At the factory they met the manager, a Mr Foster, an unassuming and polite Englishman. At that time he was a sisal manager only because of personal necessity. By nature he was a hunter. It has been said that 'Bob' Foster was one of the finest of all elephant hunters in eastern Africa. He had even been compared with the legendary 'Karamoja' Bell.

Mr Foster took his visitors round the factory which consisted of a decorticator, some brush machines, a baling press and a large diesel engine which looked badly in need of repair. He was also kind enough to give some basic economics of sisal production. Furthermore, he casually mentioned that the whole set-up, including the ten thousand acres of land, was for sale. The proprietors were in Nairobi and he gave them the address. The visitors liked what they saw so much that they forgot about their trip to Tanganyika. Instead, that night they boarded the 'One-up' to Nairobi.

Sixty thousand pounds was good money by any standard in those days. It took one day to negotiate the sale of the estate with its owner, a prominent British company. It took an additional day for the Nairobi bank to criss-cross telegrams to its Uganda branch regarding money transfers. There was only a minor hitch towards the end. The bank manager was not entirely sure if the junior partner with the clumsy looking topee would be able to sign the documents in English.

The new owners of the plantation bought a brand new Ford Mercury car in Nairobi and drove back towards Voi. In the twilight before dawn they stood in front of a huge, double-storey house, in the 'midst of nowhere'.

That was in March 1947.

They settled down to learn the basics of operating a sisal estate. They informed their families back in Uganda of the new development and indicated that they were likely to be away for a few months. Although the sisal plantation and its processing were new to them, their knowledge of machinery and labour management were great assets. Mr Foster was very useful in guiding them, too. He was also candid about his own future.

'I have worked on sisal for many years now, and, with the small savings I have I want to go back to hunting. There are too many huge "tuskers" around to resist temptation.'

'Tusker' is the term used in eastern Africa for an elephant with large tusks . . . and the partners understood.

The young cook-cum-general servant called Balisha was a Godsent gift to them, although he was no culinary master. In the evening when the two of them came home tired and dusty Balisha made sure that a hot bath was ready for them. Also awaiting them, ready laid out on the verandah, was the tea-table, over which the two sat, smoked and talked of God knows what.

There were many odd jobs to be done, loose ends to be tied up . . . And the partners improvised enterprisingly and felt mildly smug about it. The junior partner got his eldest son, Jeff, to come and help them. But, being new to the place there were two factors they had not anticipated.

It was the misfortune of the inheritors of this plantation to be confronted by devastating and prolonged droughts that plagued the area from time to time. During these droughts the whole area would be barren of vegetation, save sturdy but shrivelled sisal plants.

Then would come the marauding elephants. In hundreds. Sometimes in thousands. In a matter of weeks the thirsty and hungry elephants would attack that only surviving vegetation until, where sisal blocks once stood, there would be nothing but bare red soil which, during strong easterly winds, would blow skywards in great whirlwinds.

One morning the junior partner went to have his bath after a very hearty breakfast. When he had not come out of the bathroom half an hour later, Jeff became apprehensive. Getting no response to his calls, Jeff broke a window. His father was fully dressed and had his hand on the handle of the door in readiness to open it. His head and part of his shoulders were leaning over the chest of drawers next to the door. He could have been dead about fifteen minutes.

The dead partner had started his career with practically no formal education. In his teens he was a watch repairer. He picked up English from his more fortunate friends in his local football team. Once he successfully applied for a job as a court clerk. During his six years in that capacity he learnt to read and write the language as well as could be expected. He started reading Macaulay's works on English history and Lin Yutang's view on Christianity. Mathematics came naturally to him. In his later occupation as a lorry driver to his father's coffee-buying business he also learnt about engines and machines.

One factor strongly influenced his life – his relationship with his mother was more like that between friends than a mother and son. The woman was neither a restless nor an idle person. Her hands constantly remained occupied doing one chore or the other as she patiently talked to her son. She had lost six grown-up children through illness of accident, had been mellowed by the adversities of life and had learnt to resign herself to her fate. To her the omnipotent factors of life were righteousness and her work. Part of her nature was dripped to her son during the course of their thick bond.

He was forty four years old when he died.
His name was G.P. Visram.
He was my father.

The sisal plantation which my father had bought and the house in which he died had its beginnings some decades back. Soon after the turn of the century there was a slow but steady influx of foreigners in the British East African Protectorate of Kenya. Controversial Colonel Ewart Grogan had walked from the Cape to Cairo in a bid to convince his prospective father-in-law that he was a man of substance. En route he had passed through and had come back to settle here, convincing his friends back home to do the same. Lord Delamere was another Britisher who settled in this part of the world, and a hard-working practical man with vision. He advocated that his kith and kin in England should come and settle in this country with temperate climate and fertile land and was the pioneer of white settlement. The beginning was not easy for the new settlers. If in a particular year the drought did not hurt them, then cattle virus disease was there to settle the score. However, they struggled and survived and even prospered.

At about the same time, a metre gauge railway line was laid from Mombasa harbour on the Indian Ocean to a point on Lake Victoria. They named the terminal Port Florence in honour of the wife of the chief engineer-in-charge of construction.

This terminal was later to be known as Kisumu. The

Uganda Railway, over six hundred miles long, ripped open the country. Areas adjacent to the railway became small villages and then towns, even a city, catering for the farming and business communities.

To do the manual work of building this line the authorities brought labourers from India. Hundreds of these Indians were involved in this Herculean task of breaking open small hills, filling up ravines and constructing viaducts so that the iron track could be laid on a reasonably straight and level terrain. Heavy earth-moving equipment was yet to be invented and hammer, chisel and human muscle did most of the jobs. The workmen struggled with their masters to see the completion of the line. In some quarters it was referred to as the 'Lunatic Line'. Looking back at the history of this country nothing could be more paradoxical.

However, many of these Indian labourers did not survive to see the completion of the job. Malaria, dysentery and black-water fever took care of that. They were buried where they fell, while the iron snake penetrated deeper into Africa. Their graves, at some obscure stations – Kiyulu, Kanga, Kenani – have been obliterated by the passage of time.

Other victims were in no need of graves. They were the ones who were picked up in the dead of night by man-eating lions. A torn piece of garment found in the bush invariably explained a mysterious disappearance.

'*Rehamat Wallimohamed passed on to a better world last Saturday. We organised a decent burial service as was required of us. The ceremony was conducted by . . .* ' A long-travelled note from a friend or a sympathiser would reach a remote village in India. The bereaved family would then submit to God's will and pray for his soul. At night the widow and her children would huddle together and cry silently. No more rupees would be coming home across the ocean either, they understood . . .

Since the modern Railway Museum in Nairobi does not depict a 'coolie' being carried away from his tent by a man-eater the contemporary commuter sipping his gin and tonic on the nightly train between Mombasa and Nairobi has no way of knowing that the coach carrying him rolls over the very ground where, decades back, blood was spilt and souls were lost in the process of developing this part of the continent.

At around this time a prominent British company obtained a concession to process fibre from wild plants called San Zaveira. They grew in abundance around a railway point called Voi in south-eastern Kenya. To oversee the establishment and operation of this venture the company delegated a young Englishman fresh from 'home'. Young Albert was a meticulous and level-headed person. His craving for adventure was only matched by his liking for wide open bushlands. His wealthy parents with their double-barrelled name wanted their only child to undergo some foreign experience before taking over their own estate in a prestigious part of the English countryside. So Albert was sent to this part of the British possessions.

The young man got down to work. A fibre decorticator and other allied machinery had already been imported. He started building the factory about half a mile away from the Voi river. Within six months the factory was ready.

There was a big celebration the day the factory was opened. All the directors together with their friends and wives, travelled to witness the event. San Zaveira leaves were brought in from the bush on ox carts and fed into the decorticator. From the rear end of the machine came out milk-white fibre. They all clapped and opened champagne bottles which were passed around. Scores of local people who had gathered at some respectable distance watched the ceremony, some in amusement, some in surprise, some in disbelief, and yet some more with misgivings. Everything these foreigners did was not necessarily good, some elders thought. In any event, why were they being so noisy and clapping their hands and drinking their *pombe* direct from the bottle, they all wondered. Most unbecoming for white people!

The directors decided to grow a small acreage of sisal on a trial basis. These plants had been grown successfully in German East Africa (later to become Tanganyika and now Tanzania) across the border since Dr Richard Hindorf brought some two thousand plants of sisal from Florida, USA in 1893. Sixty-four of them survived the voyage. That humble beginning led to large areas of sisal being grown around the Usambara Mountains in that country.

The sisal venture directors in Kenya dictated that houses be built immediately for senior staff. For the manager's house Albert selected an elevated piece of land at the foot of Voi Hill. He could not have chosen a better site. The place had a commanding view of the wide basin below, surrounded by hills on practically all sides. The main railway line dissected the basin right across, a mile and a half down the site. Labour and materials were cheap in those days and this huge double-storey house was speedily built on the slopes of the hill. It had a three-foot wide wall but, since the white man possessed guns, did not give a damn about wildlife, and cared even less about devils or evil spirits, what it was meant to keep away was anyone's guess. A track led straight down to the factory two miles below, and another, passing in front of the house, was the main caravan route from the port of Mombasa to the interior. If one took this track and travelled about a mile in an easterly direction one would come across the office of the district administrator-cum-Justice of the Peace. In front of the office stood a flag-pole where, with clockwork regularity, a Union Jack was hoisted in the morning and pulled down at dusk – a small piece of coloured cloth, reminding the occasional passerby that this vacant corner of the earth was part of the mighty British Empire. In another corner, Albert's disproportion-ately huge house stood in awkward contrast to the empty wilderness of the country that surrounded it as far as the eye could see.

Soon after Albert started his fibre factory his parents insisted on his coming home to get married. He took a few months' leave and sailed for England, via Bombay in India. During the brief stopover the young man made the most tragic mistake of his life. He fell in love with an Anglo-Indian girl he met socially. They got married and sailed straight back to Kenya. This event shattered his parents, who wrote to him saying he should never show his face to them again.

A few months later the marriage itself began to falter. African bushland was no place for a chick of Bombay. Many times Albert would wake up at night to catch is wife peering outside the bedroom window into the lifeless darkness. Then she took to drinking heavily. Later on she started befriending some men at the railway station. Albert would come home in the evening to be told that *memsahib* had gone to see friends. He would dine alone and go to sleep. She invariably turned up late, but he soon found out there was no point in arguing with an intoxicated woman.

Once she came home later than usual. She staggered up the steps and into the bedroom. Albert was hanging by a rope tied to the ceiling beam. He was dead to his worldly pains and his wife sailed back to Bombay – presumably to rejoin her cocktail circuit.

ONE

Ten years after my father died in the house built by Albert, the Englishman of tragic fate, destiny led my elder brother Rustam and myself to manage the sisal plantation. Our father's senior partner's lungs finally revolted against his habit of incessant smoking and one day refused to function altogether. So, since one does not normally go getting buried wearing a felt hat the man and his precious possession were at last parted. His son had better business sense than my family. He sold us the late man's shares in the company.

In our late teens and fresh out of high school we knew as much about sisal as we knew of salami. We travelled to Voi from Uganda by train, a journey that took two days and almost two nights of peering out of a second class compartment window. At four o'clock in the morning we stepped down on a practically deserted platform. Two linesmen were going about with signal lamps in their hands. About a dozen kerosene pressure lamps were swinging from poles along the platform. The wind was cold.

'God, this place is desolate,' I said to Rustam. 'Is this where we are going to spend our lives?'

The outgoing manager of the plantation was at the station to receive us and drove us in his battered Chevrolet to the house. It was bush and jungle all the way from the station.

'I don't like it here,' I said to Rustam as soon as we reached the huge house.

'Be patient,' Rustam replied. 'Once we have made a few millions we will get our own manager to run the place for us so we can go away - maybe go to Mombasa, buy a small dinghy and take up fishing.'

Within the first year of my stay at Voi I was to realize that even if I waited for more than an eternity there would be no manager coming - let alone millions.

Within twenty hours of our arrival the outgoing manager started coaching the two of us on how to 'operate' a sisal plantation. 'There is nothing to it really,' he told us as he took us around the factory.

'Make sure each sisal cutter cuts twenty-five leaves to a bundle, and a hundred bundles, to qualify for his task of the day. However, you must be careful about one thing. From time to time, hold a wooden stick upright in the waste drain behind the decorticator. If the drain gets blocked by sisal wastes because of obstruction caused by the stick shout at the engineer. He is running his machine too sharp.'

From then on poor Mr. Jarnail Singh, the engineer, lived a life of utter misery. Every few hours he would find us at the waste drain with a wooden stick in our hand. We seemed to believe that the entire secret of running a successful sisal estate consisted in poking a stick in the waste drain and getting your engineer to rectify the problem.

'The amount of waste depends on the place from where the sisal is being cut. Most of all it depends on the weather. The drier it gets, the tougher a sisal leaf becomes and you have to scrub it harder to remove the pulp, thus causing greater amounts of waste.'

'No, Jarnail Singh, we are not satisfied with your reasoning,' we told him as once more we poked the stick into the drain. He shook his head slowly in resignation. Jarnail Singh must have cursed his God for sending two teenage idiots as his masters. He finally left the job and I doubt if he ever forgave us.

Our allowing Jarnail Singh to go was a mistake we were to regret in times to come. He belonged to the Sikh community, who are some of the finest craftsmen, technicians and engineers. They are also a very frank people.

Two days before the outgoing manager departed, leaving the estate in our care, he mentioned casually the wild animals that caused damage to sisal plants.

'Worst are the baboons and the elephants. Baboons are easier to control. Just place guards on the perimeter of the plantation at regular intervals and the baboon family will be chased away if the guard is alert.'

(Later, however, we noticed that despite posting the baboon guards, enormous amounts of sisal leaves were being eaten away. Since the only explanation for this was that at the time of damage they were attending to nature's call, we began to suspect that every baboon guard must be suffering from biological misbehaviour of the highest degree.)

'The case of elephants is a different story,' the outgoing manager went on, 'for sometimes they cannot be chased away, in which case they have to be shot.'

Rustam and I listened to him attentively. This was something we had neither heard about, nor expected.

'Mind, they can be quite destructive if left unchecked,' he continued, 'but since the company has a resident hunter you should not worry much.'

He was referring to Mr Spallino who he had introduced to us the previous day. We were not quite sure at that time what a hunter had got to do with the running of a sisal plantation. Perhaps to see that a stray leopard did not get into the labour camp, we thought. That assumption was the outer limit of our logical thinking.

'Since he has just come and there have not been any movements of elephants for quite some months, I don't know how good he is. He says he has done some hunting

15

in Rhodesia. Elephants come only during certain months of the year. Either when they are migrating from one territory to another, or when it is too dry to find any vegetation elsewhere. Oh yes, they can be quite destructive if left unchecked.'

Two days later the manager was gone. 'Don't forget the waste drain,' were his parting words.

In time to come we were to learn how important a hunter was for sisal plantation in districts with wild game around, especially the area that bordered what was then known as the Royal Tsavo National Park. But it was to be many years later and after much financial loss and breaking of morale that we were to learn how destructive an African elephant could be.

After the caretaker manager had gone, we shifted to the ground floor of the house. That night I suddenly woke up. The windows were rattling and the bedroom door was vibrating. I pushed Rustam out of his bed.

'Get up. We are having an earth tremor.'

Rustam got up and saw what was happening. We simply flew out into the driveway. The two of us stood watching the house, fright written all over our faces, and our hair standing on end. The night watchman, an elderly person with a wise look, came along and joined us looking towards the house, somewhat curiously. After a while the rattling ceased and we walked back in and went to sleep.

The next night I was just beginning to sink into sleep when the windows again began to rattle, and the doors started vibrating. I again got Rustam out of bed and we dashed into the driveway.

'What a coincidence. Two nights in a row!' I commented.

The watchman came along and stood by us again. He looked at us, then he looked at the house. Then he looked at us, thoroughly perplexed. When the rattling and shaking passed away we walked back to the house. The watchman just stood there, not shifting his eyes from us.

16

On the third night it was Rustam who pushed me out of bed and the house when the windows and doors started rattling.

'Is God going to continue throwing this at us every night?' I protested.

The watchman came along. He asked us a question.

'I know it is rude of me to ask, but do you two suffer from some nervous problem?'

'What do you mean by that?' I queried.

'Night after night I see you dashing out of the house trembling, perspiring and looking frightened to death, as you stand looking at the house.'

'Damn it, it is no nervous disorder. It's those blooming earth tremors which keep on chasing us,' I complained.

He kept looking at me searchingly while I added, 'Don't you know what earth tremors are? Look at those windows rattling. This could be followed by a full-size earthquake. Then the house could fall down. Then we all get killed.' I felt I had to put this to him in simple language.

When he realized what our panic was all about, he smiled broadly and said, 'Bwana, there are no earth tremors around here. We have rocky terrain underneath. The house only shakes a little every time a heavy goods train pushes uphill down there,' he explained, pointing to the light of a freight train heading towards Nairobi a mile away.

Rustam and I walked back to the house sheepishly.

The next night as we went to bed, I commented, 'At least tonight we can sleep undisturbed. Sleep, peaceful sleep. What was it Shakespeare said about sleep?'

'Sleep is in the mind of the beholder, I think.' Rustam replied.

'That's right,' I confirmed. 'Who could have put it more beautifully? He was a genius.'

From then on we slept peacefully. That is, for next nine nights. On the tenth night a loud ear-shattering noise followed by shock waves threw us both out of beds, broke the window panes and sent furniture floating around.

'Bloody hell! What type of trains do they operate in this country!'Rustam cried as we ran out.

Outside in the driveway the wise-looking watchman joined us, trembling, perspiring and looking frightened to death. His hair was standing on end too.

Of all nights it had to be this when the military's ammunition depot at the far end of the plantation accidentally blew off sky high!*

Altogether, everything was beginning to make us feel exhilerated. Ten thousand acres of land; three hundred workers – that was some change from school days a little time back!

At school we were insignificant. (My class teacher doubted if I would amount to anything more than a lifelong liability to society. The school headmaster moved around with a leather cane of which he made liberal use at the slightest excuse. The sadist never knew how much it hurt!) At this new place we almost began to feel like tribal chiefs.

The feeling of happiness was elevated even higher when soon after our arrival at Voi we received 'Certificate of Merit' from the District Agricultural Committee, placing our plantation as the second best in the district. We were about to frame this certificate for display in our office when Sheriff, the field assistant, told us politely not be asses. We were placed second best because there were only two plantations in the district.

Domestic life was also happy. Balisha took good care of us. His favourite dish for us was fried beef with mashed potatoes. The latter consisted of boiled potatoes with jackets

---

*('I was a junior officer in 55 Field Squadron Royal Engineers at the time of the explosion,' a Mr Peter Head of Nottingham in the UK was to write to me many years later about this explosion. 'One young soldier was killed and Second in Command was badly burnt').

removed. He would then give them a thorough beating with an old sledgehammer.

One day he made a suggestion:

'You should have your breakfast in bed. Bwana Foster used to do that, and I am told, with the exception of Major Layzell all the previous managers had their breakfast in bed.'

'But Balisha, we are quite capable of walking to the table each morning.'

'It is not a matter of being able to walk to the table; it is a question of tradition.'

We pondered for a while at this novel style of life. Might as well give it a try, we concluded. It turned out to be a difficult habit to adopt.

Next morning we got up early as usual and waited expectantly for our breakfast trays. About fifteen minutes elapsed and Balisha had not yet shown up. One of us gave in to temptation and rushed to the bathroom, brushed teeth and had his first cigarette. He was back in bed in time for the tray.

The following morning both of us were a little more daring.

We had enough time to shave and get almost ready before we slipped back into bed. In fact, on the third day Balisha found us completely dressed and ready to go to work, yet still in our beds, smoking and impatiently awaiting the breakfast trays.

'Breakfast in bed is beginning to lose its meaning if you behave like this. This is not what the other Bwanas used to do.' Balisha had a look of disappointment on his face.

'Balisha, we do not know how the old master of the plantation got indoctrinated into this early morning ritual, but it is not doing much good to either our stomachs or our nerves. As from tomorrow can we have our breakfast like other normal human beings – at the table?'

Thankfully Balisha relented.

The outgoing manager left behind a pair of dogs. 'They are brilliant guard dogs,' he told us.

Some kind of guard dogs they turned out to be.

Every evening as Rustam and I sat on the verandah the dogs almost grafted themselves to us, their tails stuck rigidly between their legs. They stared with wide open eyes in all directions in some sort of perpetual apprehension. Whenever a train passed down below and blew a whistle sharply, or if a branch of a tree snapped in the wind with a cracking noise, the two of them would dash at lightning speed under the nearest bed inside the house. Once there, they would stretch their front paws and bury their heads.

'What the hell are they doing?' I once asked Rustam.

'I have a feeling that they are desperately praying.'

A few months later they suddenly disappeared. The story got round that our guard dogs had themselves been stolen . . .

It was wise to keep quiet about that.

On his departure the outgoing manager also arranged for a new cook for us. He turned up about fifteen days later bearing the ex-manager's letter of introduction. Simon Wanjala was his name, but we dared not call him by his first name. He was in his mid-fifties and was tall and broad-shouldered. Attired in a clean white jacket, black bow tie, black trousers and black shoes, with a shine that one would only find in modern commercials, he absolutely rejected the idea of speaking in any language other than English. If you said something in Kiswahili he would stare at you questioningly, as if he had been addressed in Chinese. He could have stepped down from the pages of *Gone with the Wind*. His testimonials made it evident that he had been a cook for District Commissioners, besides other respectable masters. Balisha sat squatting on the ground at a far corner, watching us interview Mr Wanjala, knowing his powers were being usurped. As we were in need, or so we thought at that time, of a good cook, we decided to engage him. Salary and other terms of employment were settled and he was given his quarters. Next day he started to work.

That evening, as we were settling down to tea, Balisha brought us a piece of paper.

'Your cook has given me this for you.' There was a distinct tone of sarcasm. Staring at Balisha in some bewilderment Rustam took the piece of paper from his hand. It was the menu for the evening meal. On the top right hand corner was the date. Under the date was written 'VOI', lest we forget in what geographical part of the country we were dining.

It was a four-course dinner:

1. Creme de Solani with spring vegetable
2. Devil on Horseback
3. Fruits of Eden
4. Coffee
or
Tea

'Thank you Balisha,' I said.

Balisha did not move. Obviously he had something on his mind.

'What is your problem?'

'I do not want to be offensive, but in this short time I have been with you I have a feeling that your knowledge of using what cutlery for which dish is somewhat limited. You see, Bwana, your Mr Wanjala may get upset if you dip the spoon meant for fruit into the soup.'

We were grateful to him for his guidance and listened to as many tips on table manners as he knew, or thought he knew...

At eight o'clock we were summoned to dinner.

As Rustam came to sit at the table he almost tumbled down to the floor. He was ignorant of the fact that it was customary for the waiter (Mr Wanjala in this case) to pull back the diner's chair to ease him into it.

Mr Wanjala walked a few feet away and stood erect with arms folded, like a genie awaiting his master's command, while Balisha was to ferry the food from the kitchen.

Creme de Solani with spring vegetable turned out to be tomato soup reeking with raw onions. In the next few days we learnt that 'spring vegetable' invariably meant raw onions. Ever since then I have never seen Rustam being able to come within two yards of any onion, reeking or not.

As soon as the soup was finished, Balisha appeared with the next dish, *Devil on Horseback*. Each plate consisted of three mingy pieces of toasted bread with baked beans sparingly spread over them. We even surreptitiously licked the trace of sauce left on the plate. Once more Balisha appeared as if summoned by a secret signal from Mr Wanjala. In his hand he held the *Fruits of Eden*.

All this was happening without a word being exchanged between the four of us. Mr Wanjala was still standing in position, arms folded, to see that everything was going well, while Rustam and I sat rigidly in our chairs. *Fruits of Eden* consisted of local pawpaw so botched up that it could have been passed through a meat mincer over and over again. It was topped by two tiny bits of sweet banana – half ripe at that. We apologised to Mr Wanjala for not being interested in either coffee or tea. That was the end of the dinner.

Some of the workers coming out from the late shift from the factory must have wondered why the new managers were hanging around Patel's Café so late at night, drinking tea from mugs and hurriedly downing samosas.

Next morning the cook told us to have the car sent up to him so that he could go shopping. And so it was sent to him. Mr Wanjala sat in the back seat. Next to the driver in the front seat was Balisha, holding a shopping basket and looking like a licked puppy.

That evening for curiosity's sake we went to the kitchen to see what our well-meaning cook had bought. Our eyes nearly popped out of their sockets. That was no kitchen –

it was a mini supermarket! There were piles upon piles of tins, packets and other assorted containers. Different types of cheese, tins of olives, scores of packets of soup, tartar sauce . . . chilli sauce . . . sweet and sour sauce . . . any type of sauce . . . margarine, golden syrup. The list could have been endless.

Rustam and I walked out of the kitchen wondering if the situation was getting out of hand. The man had even arranged for his personal standard to be hoisted over the kitchen door. You could ask for tea or sandwiches as long as the blue flag was up. Once the red flag was flying, you could collapse from starvation, without getting so much as a few breadcrumbs. But there was more to come.

'Do you have a tie?' Balisha asked me one day.

'A tie?'

'Yes, a necktie.'

'No. Why do you want to know?'

'Once or twice Mr Wanjala has enquired if the bwanas might have neckties.'

Rustam, who had overheard the conversation, asked, 'Why should a cook want to know if his masters possess neckties?'

'I haven't got the foggiest idea,' I replied.

Not until many years later, when once I got dumped out of a Mombasa hotel where I had gone for dinner in shirtsleeves, did I learn the relationship between tie and dinner and know what designs Mr Wanjala had in mind.

From that night on we never found out what we were eating. The basic food content was craftily camouflaged by other ingredients. To add to the confusion all the menus were made out in unprounceable French. We ate what was served, obediently, quietly and sufferingly.

The crux came when we received the grocer's monthly account.

'Mr Wanjala, do you enquire about the price of any item before you buy it?'

'I am a cook, not a cashier, Sir.'

'Then, let us enlighten you about some financial facts,' Rustam replied, trying to control his anger. 'Between the two of us, our salaries total shillings two thousand and four hundred a month. Your grocery bill has come to shillings two thousand, one hundred forty and eighty cents. We are left with about two hundred and sixty shillings to get through the next month!'

There was a pregnant pause, while Simon Wanjala stood erect with no expression on his face.

'You better GO!' Rustam was in no mood to mince his words.

Next day Simon Wanjala packed up and left in search of service to more sophisticated masters. Before leaving he said to Balisha that these masters were a very primitive type of people and he saw little future for them in modern colonial Kenya.

TWO

In the beginning it was difficult to manage the plantation. As time passed by it became nearly impossible.

There was much more to it than counting the number of leaves per bundle and watching the waste drain. There was a perpetual shortage of sisal cutters and they had to be recruited from the other end of the country. Production targets had to be kept. Old sisal fields had to be uprooted and new ones planted. Petty quibbles amongst junior staff had to be sorted out.

Then there were the outside forces:

LABOUR INSPECTORS had to be satisfied about the welfare of their workers.

'We are not very happy about the safety record at your place. There is a man lying in hospital with broken ribs,' once the labour inspector complained over the telephone.

We replied. "The bushfire watch should not have tied one end of the rope to his belly and the other to his grazing bull. They like to chase passing by cows. This business of 'opposite sex atracts' was all started by Sigmund Freud. We deny any responsibility."

The labour inspector muttered something about the world becoming madder and madder before replacing his receiver.

BANK MANAGER: In order to stretch our credit a little more he had to be told how smart and how clever his child was.

(Personally, I had yet to see a more stupid looking brat, always picking his nose.)

AGRICULTURE OFFICERS: They had to be kept informed about progress. We invited one and took him around, enthusiastically explaining our future programmes and modes of planting. He listened without making any comment. Before leaving he puffed on his pipe while looking towards the sky and said: 'There are two sad aspects about this place: The first one is that you don't know anything about agriculture, the second is that you don't know that you don't know anything about agriculture.'

'Cheeky swine!' I commented when he had gone.

FACTORY INSPECTORS had to be coped with. There was a small mishap with the first factory inspector who ever called on us. He had driven from Mombasa accompanied by a lady. He found fault with every machine: the transmission belt was too old; the air receivers were overdue for check-up by six weeks; the guard of a pully was too weak . . . He went on thundering at us for hours while entering each item in his book.

As we sat in the office after the inspection he started quoting one section after another of Factory Law under which we could be prosecuted and punished severely. He said that incompetence had its own limits and we would be more at home with the Salvation Army than connected to any factory.

'The factory will have to remain closed until all these matters have been rectified. You shall be receiving my official letter as soon as I arrive back in my office in Mombasa,' he said. He waited while we turned off various machines.

For fifteen minutes after he had gone we sat in silence wondering what to do next. This was a hard blow to us. We did not know how to meet the production target and what to do with the idle labour force.

'I know what to do,' Rustam had the solution. 'Since he

26

has not instructed us in writing to stop operating the factory, let us start the machines up again. By now he should be miles away on his way to Mombasa.' Immediately the place was throbbing with life once more.

Not half an hour had elapsed before the factory inspector's car reappeared in the compound. Apparently he had left his expensive Parker pen on our table and only remembered it while having tea at the nearby Park Inn.

'You bloody idiots, you bloody, bloody idiots,' he shouted trembling with anger. 'At least you should have had the decency to give me a couple of hours' start before re-operating your machines behind my back. I will see that you never run your factory again . . . I will see that you are ruined . . . I will see that you are never employed by any industry in this country. I will see that . . .' He stopped there without finishing the sentence.

'He has run out of punishments,' Rustam whispered to me timidly.

That evening as we sat on the verandah Rustam commented: 'The man was mighty angry!'

'No wonder he was angry,' I said. 'You should have known better than to tell him to let his mother rest in the office while we inspected the machines!'

'How was I to know the old wrinkled thing in his car was his wife!'

That year the rains did not come towards the end of March as they normally do in Kenya. In fact the rains failed to materialise even in April, which is supposed to be the wettest month of the 'long rains' as the season is called. Soft white clouds just floated shamelessly around the sky. The month of May saw some rain, but not enough to sustain sisal plants for the next six months or so of dry season which follows the long rains. That month Rustam and I also had our first encounter with elephants.

It happened on a Saturday morning. Mwagudu, the company's tracker, brought in a report that some elephant foot-prints were seen not very far from our house. Mwagudu had worked for the company since he was a child. He was old now, but his tall and lean body had the swiftness of a leopard. Hunting was in his blood since he was born of the Wariangulu tribe which thrives on meat of wild animals. In his particular field he had the wisdom of Solomon. Mr Spallino, our hunter, was informed of the elephants' proximity.

And shoot the elephants he did. But he made a very messy job of it. He used sixteen bullets and took six hours to accomplish it. Later we were to learn that he had parked his vehicle about a thousand feet from the creature from where he took pot-shots at the huge target from time to time, returning quickly back to his vehicle's cab after every shot . . . just in case. The first shot must have injured one leg of the animal very badly because he could not move far. He was condemned to keep on taking the beating from this unkind hunter.

It was Spallino's misfortune to be in our office when the game warden entered in an extremely foul temper. He grabbed Spallino's shirt collar and pushed him into a chair.

'Where did you learn your shooting anyway? Most likely in the Abyssinian war. Every time you were supplied with guns you artistic-minded race cut off their barrels and made flutes out of them to play your music.' The English game warden was incensed by Spallino. 'Sixteen blooming bullets! By Jove, sixteen blooming hard-nosed bullets! Surely it must be some kind of a record for elephant shooting – one eyeball shattered, both front teeth broken, left ear torn off, tail blown off. By Jove, couldn't you find one vital spot? Did you see his trunk? It has been mutilated to resemble a Victorian lady's bloomers. There is no law in this country as to how many rounds should be spent to kill an animal. Pity! Sixteen blooming bullets!'

Later Mwagudu was frank over the issue. 'The man was

clearly scared, Bwana. He would not come within three hundred yards of the creature. You better watch out, Bwana.'

A few days after Mr Spallino resigned to take up 'some new opening in Ethiopia.' We were not entirely sorry to see him leave.

We noticed the baboon menace was somehow getting out of control. Posting extra baboon guards did not improve the situation.

Then Naran came to us with a suggestion for our baboon problem. He worked in the clerical section of the office, a small man with big ideas. His idea to teach the baboons a lesson turned out to be the right solution and we shifted him from the office to the carpentry shed to launch his anti-baboon campaign – coded Red Devil.

He was supplied with red paint, some strong sticking agent and thinner. Then he ordered a few trappers to trap baboons into steel cages – a very difficult job. The cages containing baboons, one in each, were brought to the factory. Naran would fill a four-gallon tin halfway up with red paint, mix in plenty of sticking agent and add a pint of thinner for a quick drying effect. Then the mixture would be poured over the somewhat baffled and protesting baboon.

The cages would be taken back to the baboon colony and the creature set free. It would run to join its colleagues. The others would not only not accept the devilish looking creature amongst them, but would panic into running the hell away from it. The red baboon would run behind them and they would run even further away. In a matter of hours they would have all disappeared into the faraway hills.

'Bravo, Naran, bravo!'

He was pleased and felt proud.

One day there was a catastrophe. There were three cages containing baboons to be treated. Naran got down on the floor to prepare his formula. As he rose again afterwards, he accidentally knocked down a tin containing ready 'charge' on the shelf behind him. The liquid came down, pouring all over him. He stood there, totally stunned.

People began to gather around the carpentry shed to witness a most unusual sight. The decorticator gang was there; people from the garage were there; 'brushers' were there. By the time we reached the scene, the crowd had swollen. In their midst stood Naran, very stunned and as still as a statue under the paint. The onlookers were sympathetically quiet, except for occasional exclamations of, 'Aye aye ya – aye aye ya!'

Nature created white man. Nature created black man. Nature created brown man. Nature even created a yellow man. What Nature had never intended, we had done here at Voi – a shining bright red man. I did not know whether to laugh out loud or feel sorry, or to go to a secluded spot, fall on my knees and ask God's forgiveness for creating a new race for mankind.

Naran was taken to his quarters and given a stiff tot of brandy. The paint had dried beyond the scrubbing off point. It was decided that he should be given compassionate leave to stay with his family. He was heavily camouflaged with gloves, hat, etc, and was put on the night train to Mombasa where his family lived.

Naran said he would be back in a week or so. We never saw the man again.

It is almost sacrilegious to kill wild animals today. Not even a small dik-dik for the pot. Animal conservationists hold these sentiments with entire justification. The wild game issue is a tricky one. Population is on the rise, and, while room is being made for human settlements, animals also have been given their place of settlement. However, there have been areas where they brushed with each other, and authorities had to act very carefully at such spots. As time passed the situation began to be more and more difficult. Want for a bigger share of land by human beings is not the only factor. Poachers have played their part too. In their greed for horns and tusks they have hunted down animals mercilessly, inhumanly and without a thought for the future.

This has not always been the picture. About a century back human settlements were smaller, fewer, and farther between. Animals had almost all the land to themselves. There was not much cause for conflict between the two species. If Theodore Roosevelt, President of the United States of America, or the Crown Prince of England decided to ride on the cowcatcher of a locomotive and shoot any trophy that took their fancy there was no reason for raised eyebrows, let alone an outcry.

With the passing of time things began to change gradually and people began to expand their horizons. Not only did they grow in number but, for betterment of their living, they opened up more land. Animals were beginning to be pushed further and further afield in smaller and smaller areas. Farmers began to be vigilant about their crops, else a lion might pick up the cattle if *bomas* were not fortified. Baboons would have a field day at banana plantations. Elephants would uproot maize. Either you eliminated the animals or they would eliminate you. The Game Department was set up by the government to keep the poachers off the animals and the animals off the farms. As the years passed, the conflict took on a greater dimension. Animals, squeezed into pockets of land called either game reserves or national parks, became more daring and aggressive. By mid-century the conflict had grown into a fully fledged war between humans and animals in certain parts of the country.

It was about this time that Rustam and myself walked into one such corner of conflict. We had no stomach to kill a rat, let alone an angry she-elephant weighing three tons. We had depended on the resident hunter of the company to save the sisal fields from being run over by marauding elephants from the adjoining park, but Spallino's departure left us defenceless.

The local game warden was most helpful and he understood our plight. He seconded scouts to chase away with thunder-flashes a family of elephants that would occasionally stray into the estate. If the loud cracking of a thunder-flash did not deter the herd the warden himself saw to it that one of them was shot. That would do the trick. That particular herd would never appear again and the stench of a dead animal kept other herds at bay. Care had to be taken not to shoot the matriarchal leader of the family. She was their guide and if she died the remaining members would simply become confused and start running in different directions in panic, trampling sisal plants in their path.

Lack of rains that particular year did not make matters any easier. The months of June and July saw more frequent animal attacks and greater amounts of plants being eaten away. We were now beginning to be worried. The previous manager had been right in at least one respect when he told us, 'Keep elephants under check or they will destroy you.'

At Voi we suffered from an unpleasant fact of life. If perchance God wakes up during the night and suddenly remembers that a certain person has remained unpunished for his sin of the day He will administer an instant punishment. He will have a tiny mosquito infiltrate into the culprit's mosquito net as he sleeps. Just when you are beginning to sink into a deep slumber the enemy makes his presence felt with a buzzing noise. Not being on the electric mains, you cannot switch on the lights and locate the mosquito and crush it with a quick clap of your hands. Searching for it with a flashlight is like looking for a needle in a haystack. Once in a while you may feel it biting you in its favourite spot, the back of your ear. You give a sharp slap. Not only is the creature still loose but you have an added problem. The eardrum is now ringing madly. You spend the night half asleep, half awake. At times you get hysterical and wonder why Noah had to arrange for a pair of mosquitoes to join his ark at all.

It was on one such night of fighting a mad mosquito that I heard a car drive into the compound.

Clad in our pyjamas, Rustam and I opened the front door to find out who was paying us a call at this odd hour in a large American sedan. The vehicle was evidently past her heyday, the radiator was blowing clouds of steam and not one square yard of bodywork was free from dents. The front right-hand side of the car almost touched the ground. I thought that the springs must have been removed from the vehicle – that is, until we saw the driver come out of it. I had seldom seen a person as huge, although he could not have been more than five feet ten or so. Everything below his neck was enormous – at least three hundred pounds, I thought. He carefully planted his feet as he walked up the stairs to the verandah where we stood. He looked down at us, two tiny youngsters hardly past their twentieth birthdays.

'Is your father at home?' The visitor enquired.

'No,' I replied.

'Which will be better, wait for him now or see him in the morning?'

'Neither. You will never see him,' I said.

'Why?' He seemed confused.

'Because he has been dead many years, that is why.'

There was a look of genuine shock and embarrassment on the visitor's face. His tone was much milder when he next spoke.

'I am sorry about this mix-up. I was told that there is a job for a hunter going here.'

'That is true. Do you normally go looking for jobs at night?'

'I am sorry. The journey from Nairobi took longer than I expected.'

Then I made a remark which I regretted the instant words

had come out of my mouth. 'No wonder, with your sized body and the state of your car!'

There was a pause and I expected him to be angry or rude. Instead he laughed aloud and said, 'You know, by God, that is true.' That very instant I developed a liking for the visitor.

Thus we met our new hunter, Sher. He was provided with a company house and a Land-Rover for his control works and, for the following year and a half, was to guide and misguide our lives to the best of his ability. Until this day I am not sure what particular quality made him such an interesting person. He was a good conversationalist. One could pick on any subject and Sher would dwell on it at length. The fact that half the things upon which he professed to be an authority were products of his imagination did not bother him in the least. If ever anyone called his bluff he had the finest knack for sidetracking into another topic, usually a saucy one, without anyone realising the change. He seemed to know about every subject on our planet. He would talk about the breeding habits of Arabian horses, the latest scandal in the White House, the dowry system of the people living in Outer Mongolia, or even about the love life of William Shakespeare. He would frown into an extremely thoughtful mood as he would run his palms over his cheeks, half close his eyes and look towards the floor and say:

'The Americans have their own Rasputin in Edgar Hoover of the FBI. Pity the ordinary American does not realise this fact.'

'Who is Mr Rasputin?'

'Rasputin? Oh, I will tell you some day about that mad Russian.'

At that stage I knew very little about his private life. I once asked him: 'Are you a married person, Sher?'

'From time to time,' he replied, trying to stifle a yawn.

He also seemed to have a solution to most problems. For

example, if one suffered from piles, the best cure was to drink a mixture of dried powder of cactus flower mixed with yogurt. Gang Ram, the company's carpenter had piles problem but was very reluctant to try this unknown potion. Rustam persuaded him.

For three painful days and nights Ganga Ram winced and whimpered, twisted and turned in his bed. Then his family took him to Mombasa for treatment. His wife sent us a message from there that as soon as the surgeon had stitched her husband back to a reasonably original shape, she would personally take up the matter with The District Officer about our barbaric behaviour.

I have yet to know of a woman creating so many problems. It would be best to spare you mentioning the profanities that she hurled at us.

September. No sign of rain. More elephants ventured out of the game park to pick on the plants, which have the capacity to store more water than most vegetation – in this case, *our sisal*. Sher was discreet in his duties. Despite nightly visits by various groups of elephants he was obliged to shoot only one of them during the whole month. It belonged to a family that had got used to the loud explosions of thunder flashes kindly supplied to us by the game warden (not to be confused by the park warden whose jurisdiction was restricted to park boundaries). It was a small bull and the job was quick and swift. The rest of the family members got the message. They never came back.

The middle of the month saw some nimbus clouds forming on the horizon. They occasionally crossed from one end of the horizon to disappear on the other. In their course they would pass directly overhead, mocking the thirsty beasts, vegetation and the men below. As could be expected, Sher once again had a solution to our problem.

'It is very simple. Just sprinkle some sodium chloride on

the passing clouds. They will burst open. I am told ranchers do that up in the northern district.'

'And who is going to climb up the cloud to sprinkle your sodium chloride?'

'We can work out some solution, I am sure.' Sher was not deterred.

The next day he came up with the solution.

'Get me a large cylinder of hydrogen and plenty of balloons.'

Hydrogen gas and balloons were brought in from Mombasa. Sher got down to manufacturing his rain-making device, explaining to us as he worked on his contraption:

'A balloon of this size filled with hydrogen will ascend at a rate of two hundred feet per minute with its payload. I have already made field tests on it. If, say, a rain-bearing cloud is floating two thousand feet above us, the balloon will take ten minutes to reach it. Now, here is this cellophane bag tied under the balloon containing gunpowder and common salt.'

He had previously extracted gunpowder by carefully opening a shotgun cartridge.

'There is this fuse tied to this cellophane bag. The fuse burns at the rate of two inches every minute. When the fire reaches the bag the gunpowder will blow it up, scattering the salt all around. For impregnating a cloud two thousand feet up, for example, allow twenty inches of fuse, light it and release the balloon. Scientific principles will take over from then on.'

The inflammable nature of the hydrogen gas prohibited us from keeping a stock of ready-inflated balloons. Therefore Sher's Land-Rover was fitted with various paraphernalia for rain-making: the gas cylinder, dozens of balloons, rolls of fuses, bags of common salt, gunpowder. The vehicle was stationed near the office, as alert as a fire engine. People were sent out into the fields to look out for any approaching clouds, while Sher went to bed to rest before performing the duty.

Two days later a black cloud was sighted in the easterly sky aiming towards our area. Bush telegraphy started clicking. The message was received in the office. Sher was woken up from his slumber. Mwagudu was already making sure the vehicle still carried the necessary materials. He was not entirely satisfied with his new duty, believing that the slaughtering of a black sheep in traditional fashion was a more reliable method of getting some rain. But maybe these newcomers had something up their sleeve about which he and his tribesmen were not aware.

Rustam and I were most interested in the operation. We squeezed ourselves between the other rain-makers as Sher took off in his Land-Rover in great clouds of red dust.

Sher's vehicle flew over minor ravines, jumped over small ant hills. Soon we were at the desired spot and the party came to a halt. Sher made some quick observations and with the confidence of an experienced airline pilot said the cloud seemed to be about two thousand three hundred feet high. He made another calculation and the fuse was cut to the required length. Two more fuses were cut, one a little longer, and another a little shorter. He intended to launch three balloons to burst at different heights, since he could not judge precisely the elevation of the target. Balloons were released in succession. They surged vertically up as we watched in anticipation. The first balloon passed way in front of the approaching cloud. The second and third balloons drifted sideways with the cross winds before they could hit the cloud. The clouds floated away leisurely. Nobody spoke.

'Even the best hunter misses his target occasionally.' Sher was the first to speak a little time later, but it did not go down too well with us. We drove back minus the rear bumper of the Land-Rover, which a small stump of a tree had ripped out.

This wild goose chase was repeated the next day and the next without much success. During these chases the company vehicle broke one main leaf of the spring and two spring hangers. One tyre was torn into shreds. Novelty and hope were wearing thin. On a few occasions some balloons hit the nimbus clouds, but had nothing to do with Sher's calculations or estimates. They were sheer accidents caused by the law of averages. What none of us had realised at that time was the fact that even if a balloon did penetrate a cloud the moisture would dampen the fuse, the fire, the gunpowder and the lot. That is, if Sher was to be believed that a handful of common salt can bring down a deluge of rain.

A couple of days later one promising cloud happened to be passing dead over the factory compound. Through the window of our office we watched as Sher and his team prepared to launch yet another salvo of balloons. This time he must have made a gross miscalculation in the principles of physics. The balloon rose for ten feet and then started sinking down. When it came down to about four feet above the ground it stopped sinking. Then it hovered around in the mild breeze, its fuse emitting smoke as it burnt.

The Nairobi to Mombasa road passed not very far from the factory compound. An elderly couple in their vintage Morris were on their way to the coast. The balloon gently settled on the car's bonnet, its tail still ablaze. The car jolted to a halt. Rustam and I watched the melodrama from the office window, our fists clenched.

'Get the hell out of the car, Mavis, I don't like it.' The husband was pulling the old lady out of the door. She was still busy adjusting her straw hat and trying to put her shoes on. They both disappeared into a ditch by the roadside and crouched on the ground with hands covering their heads, waiting for their car to be blown sky high any moment.

'We are going to jail for this,' Rustam commented, perspiration dripping down our foreheads.

As soon as the fuse was spent, the sparks reached the bag. There was a small muffled explosion as the gunpowder caught fire, discharging the salt. The balloon, now having jettisoned its payload, shot straight into the sky. The old man and his lady partner approached their car after a reasonable interval. Luckily they did not report the matter to the authorities. Or, if they did, the local police commander, Superintendent Hopkins, did not refer back to us.

By now many people around the district had observed us hurling strange objects towards heaven. However, no one was quite sure what it was all about. One village elder told his people that we were probably sending secret messages to God.

'No, that is not true." A younger person contradicted. 'I tell you these people have gone plain loony.'

Yet another was adamant that we were members of a strange and mysterious religious cult that performed such rituals every summer. "I TELL YOU, THAT FAT MAN (meaning Sher) IS THEIR HIGH PRIEST". He was quite hysterical in his accusations.

One day the District Officer summoned Rustam and Sher to his office. 'What is all this I hear about sending balloons into the open sky?

Sher began. 'I am glad that our efforts for the benefits of the local community are beginning to be noticed and appreciated. You see, you cut a fuse about four inches long….'.

'Stuff the fuses down your throat.' The District Officer was bursting with anger. 'You should be ashamed of yourselves, playing around with balloons like small kids'.

'It is sad.' Sher closed his eyes, remorse written all over his face. 'How can a noble deed not be appreciated?'

The District Officer said, 'There is a communication from the Civil Aviation Authority in Nairobi.   Pilots of small aircrafts flying over our district are puzzled and apprehensive at the sight of scores of bright red balloons floating aimlessly. They want to know what the hell is happening.' The District Officer shouted, fire belching from his nostrils. 'STOP THAT AT ONCE.'

I am told that when the rains finally came, Mwagudu slaughtered a black sheep and offered it to his God. He was grateful to the Almighty that he did not have to be a party to this insane behaviour.

THREE

'We are having some problem in one of our wheel tractors.' It was the chief mechanic's assistant from the company's garage. 'There is a grinding noise in the gearbox.'

'Why don't you get Lofty to look into it?' Lofty was the nickname of the chief mechanic. He was over six foot tall.

'Bwana, Lofty is attending his mother-in-law's funeral,' said the assistant.

'But he attended his mother-in-law's funeral only a couple of weeks back!' Rustam was more inquisitive than annoyed. There was a brief pause before Rustam spoke again. 'Coming to think of it, I distinctly remember about six months ago he took a few days off to attend his mother-in-law's funeral. Does the old lady keep reincarnating too quickly or what?'

The assistant remained quiet.

'Come on, let us soil our hands once in a while. After all, what is it? It is only a gearbox,' I said to Rustam.

The three of us walked to the garage. The assistant and his two spanner boys removed the gearbox housing from the belly of the tractor. We then asked them to open the inspection cover. It did not give much clue to the malady. Someone with even basic knowledge of mechanics would have found out the cause of the trouble at this stage. We asked the assistant and his two mates to disassemble the whole gearbox. This they did while we stood over them.

Now all the gears were naked to our eyes. One had to be blinking blind not to recognize that one of the gears was badly worn out.

'You see, this is the trouble.' There was a tone of chastisement as we waved the worn-out gear at the three juniors. They looked at it with blank eyes.

The part number of the gear was relayed over the phone to the tractor's servicing agents in Mombasa. Next morning the new gear was in our factory. Rustam and I got down to putting the gearbox right. Three juniors helped us as different parts were replaced in the right position of the machine. The juniors fixed the gearbox back on the tractor while Rustam and I sat on a chair in a patronizing manner. There was no satisfaction like a job well done! The tractor was ready. It was started and we asked one of the drivers to test it. There was no longer a grinding noise coming out of the gearbox. The driver depressed the clutch pedal to keep the tractor stationary as he shifted the gear lever from one position to another. The lever moved swiftly. All seemed perfect. However there was one new problem:

The tractor had now developed four reverse speeds and only one forward speed!

Rustam looked at me and I looked back at him. The tractor driver and three garage helpers looked at both of us in bewilderment. We asked them to open the whole gearbox again. All the gears were put back onto the tractor. Again the same result. It was too late to work again that day. As we were leaving and were out of the earshots of the mechanic' assistants, I could notice them making some comments in their dialect. I don't think they were very flattering observations about us.

We tried different combinations the whole of the next day, perspiration dripping from our foreheads. The lunatic tractor was addicted to its new habit.

'I am not going to spend the rest of my life pulling trailers

42

with a tractor fixed in reverse position.' The driver was the first to protest. 'Do you know what may have gone wrong?'

'We feel the agents have supplied us with a wrong part.' That was the only face-saving explanation we had to offer. The workers did not say anything, but I did not like their looks.

That night we ate in silence. 'This case is as bad as the incident of grandpa's car,' Rustam said to me before retiring.

Our grandpa was a moneylender back at Kampala in Uganda. A very clever one. One young upcoming motor mechanic called Pusho approached grandpa for a loan of three thousand pounds to expand his garage. They haggled for days before agreeing to terms of interest and repayment. The negotiations were concluded with an understanding that Pusho should carry out minor repairs on grandpa's car without charging him.

'That is no problem.' Pusho accepted.

Here Pusho made one of the silliest mistakes of his life. He should have at least seen the car before walking into such an arrangement.

The old Vauxhall was probably the first car to roll off the assembly line of its manufacturers. It had served so many masters for so many years that it could hardly be classified as a motor vehicle at all. It was more of a collection of lots of rattling metal pieces. The day the brakes did not fail, the steering system would. On a rare occasion when both functioned well, the accelerator was certain to get jammed. He who rode in this car minus an umbrella on a rainy day was a sorry soul. Once a traffic policeman, directing traffic from his wooden pedestal at a busy junction, was lucky enough to notice in time this vehicle shooting at frantic speed towards him. He jumped off and dashed onto a nearby pavement just in time to see the car toss his pedestal into the air before disappearing down the road.

Nearly every driver left our grandpa's employ within three

months. The only one who lasted for about five months gave up driving altogether and became a bus conductor.

Barely two days had gone by after the money had been lent before the car turned up at Pusho's garage.

'It is overheating.'

Pusho got it fixed.

During the same week the car was brought in twice again: the wiper was not working and on the second occasion the exhaust was leaking. The following week, likewise, it called in twice. On the first occasion there was a minor 'miss' in the engine, and on the second the handbrake was weak. But during the third week it went to the garage four times. At the end of that month Pusho began to be apprehensive, and after a further fortnight this apprehension had turned into outright rage.

The next time grandpa took his car in, complaining of a humming noise in the differential, Pusho refused to have anything to do with it.

'Do you think I am operating my garage for the sole purpose of repairing this old junk all my life?'

'Calm down my child.' Grandpa tried to subdue him. 'Life has its pitfalls.' He went on about the philosophy of life and the virtues of being patient, while subtly reminding him about the 'payment on demand' term in their money-lending transaction. Pusho stared back at him with angry eyes.

Once Pusho woke his wife during the night. 'Do you think I am as stupid as some people take me to be?'

'Go back to sleep. You are behaving strangely of late,' his wife replied.

The next time grandpa's car called in for some repairs the embittered mechanic did three things. First, he fiddled with its gearbox and fixed it in such a way that the first gear stopped functioning. It would slip out as soon as it was engaged. Secondly, he repaid grandpa his loan, having borrowed money from some other source at somewhat higher interest. Lastly, he told grandpa to get lost.

44

Normally, a malfunctioning gearbox would have been just another of the many shortcomings of this old car. One could usually get it rolling in second gear. But the city of Kampala is built on seven hills. From thereon, for a long time to come, if a car was ever seen negotiating a particularly steep section of a road in reverse, people knew whose car it was. But not many could reason out why a car should be driven in that fashion.

Our case was as pathetic as grandpa's car, I thought the next morning when we decided to call in outside help. A friend of ours in Mombasa had a friend who had a friend who was a diesel mechanic. A request was put over the telephone that night. The diesel mechanic arrived the next afternoon. Mr Deen had spent all his life at such jobs. He simply had to remove the inspection cover of the gearbox to realise what had been messed up.

'Who has done this stupid job?' he asked Rustam.

Nobody answered. He stopped working and looked at us.

'I asked. Who has done this childish job?'

'Our mechanic,' Rustam replied. 'We are fed up with this man. Anyway he is busy burying his mother-in-law.'

Our assistant mechanic, his mates and the driver all looked at the two of us. First in utter disbelief and then in silent accusation and contempt.

'He must be a bloody idiot!' came back a curt comment.

If ever a dictionary had been written on profanity, then this Mr Deen must have read it over and over again. He could even have made a small contribution to its publication. As he worked on the machine his every sentence was punctuated with swear words I never imagined existed – all of them directed to the person who had repaired the gearbox . . .

The assistant mechanic and his mates helping Deen had faint smiles on their faces. They would not make any comments now. In the privacy of the labour lines that night they were likely to have an extra helping of *booza*, the local beer. They might even offer a glass to their friends and laugh their heads off at the myth that whatever their bosses said was always right. Rustam and I stood a little away, not knowing in particular what to do.

The tractor was its original self in an hour.

'When your mechanic comes back from leave, tie him to a tree and flog him hard. Bloody idiot!' Mr Deen advised us, before boarding his bus for Mombasa.

Since then, if there were any problems of a mechanical nature, our team never referred them to us. They did the best they could, leaving the rest to Almighty God.

Not long afterwards, the maintenance of a truck was added to their care.

Mr Khan was an enterprising businessman in one of the countries neighbouring Kenya. He occasionally travelled to Mombasa on his business errands, stopping at Voi on the way. We became good acquaintances. Normally he would have tea with us before going on.

Once he arrived in the evening and we asked him to spend the night with us instead of travelling further at such a late hour. He accepted. As we sat on the upper verandah we called Balisha to tell him that there would be one more person dining with us.

'Please don't cook anything extra for me,' Mr Khan commented. 'I am a man of poor appetite.'

That night the three of us sat down to dine. Our guest with a poor appetite went over the dishes like a vacuum cleaner. He then ate bananas as if he had never seen such a delicacy. During our small talk after dinner he said he had a good seven-ton truck for sale.

'Are you replacing it with a new one?' I asked.

'Yes, that is more or less the idea. I have this sawmill. This truck is sent up to a nearby hill where most of the timber trees are. It brings down the logs. A few days ago its brakes failed on a tricky bend. It ran down a small valley, ending up in someone's garden bringing down part of the chicken shed.'

'So what?' I asked.

'So what! One does not send a fully loaded truck crashing into the Forest Officer's garden. Especially not if you are in the timber trade. The man has become very difficult lately with the issue of log permits. I have to buy a new truck for this type of work.'

That night I suggested to Rustam that we buy this truck from Mr Khan. It could collect sisal bulbils for the nursery and carry the small plants for planting. Rustam readily agreed with me. The next time Mr Khan passed Voi we told him we would buy his truck. An amount equivalent to Kenya shillings four thousand was good enough for Mr Khan in his country. There was one problem though:

'How will you get it into Kenya? Getting customs clearance and other documents is virtually impossible at my end.'

'Leave that to us,' Rustam replied.

'You know who will do the job for us,' Rustam said to me when Mr Khan had departed. I knew.

Gandhi was the odd job man on the plantation. He had one special quality. When it came to any 'crooked' dealing, Gandhi fitted into the slot like a hand into a glove. What an irony, if one were to think of the saintly figure of the Indian subcontinent!

The mission was explained to Gandhi and, without an apparent thought, he said, 'No problem!' Ten days later he travelled to Mr Khan's sawmill and took possession of the Albion truck.

So it was that, at the isolated border post of the adjoining country, an Albion truck driven by a scruffy looking person halted at the barrier gate. A customs officer came out of the cubicle and walked up to the truck. In the back was a wooden coffin, decorated with banana leaves and wild flowers and surrounded by ten sad looking mourners. In the far corner was Gandhi with a lost look on his face. Before the customs officer could ask any questions, Gandhi jumped off the truck, put his arm around the shoulder of the officer and drew him aside.

'Poor thing, cut down in the prime of his youth. Jaundice, you know!'

'I am sorry.' The customs officer was sympathetic. 'Where are you taking his body?'

'About fifteen miles across the border. His home town.' Gandhi's eyes were almost misty.

'Do you have the papers?'

Gandhi looked slightly puzzled and then quickly dug out a card from his jacket pocket.

'Here. This is my *kipande*. I suppose this is what you want!'

'No, we don't want your identity card. We need the customs papers for the truck.'

Gandhi remained puzzled for a moment. Then he sighed deeply and said, 'You don't know what trouble we have had organising this funeral and hiring this truck. Now unexpectedly you want us to produce this ... er ... customary papyrus.'

'Customs papers,' the officer corrected this illiterate person. By now a second officer had joined them. The two officers walked a few paces away and consulted each other, visibly touched by this sob story. After a while they came back to Gandhi.

'How soon will you bring the truck back?'

'Eight hours at the most.'

'This is very irregular. Come back as soon as you have finished with your business. Don't get us into any trouble.'

Gandhi shook both officers' hands warmly and repeatedly, while praying aloud that their wives might bear them lots of children, and God stand by them in times of trouble. The gate was opened and the truck allowed through, with the officers removing their caps in homage to the 'deceased'.

Ten miles inside Kenya, Gandhi disbanded the group of professional mourners and gave them a promised ten shillings each.

'Do not cross back by the customs post, you useless scoundrels. Use the bush tract,' Gandhi advised them before driving off at full speed without once looking back.

At times I wonder how long the two customs officers waited for the truck to return before beginning to feel like damned fools!

If Gandhi could outsmart customs officers, he could outsmart other people too. Once we ran short of money required for end-of-month payments to the workers. It was decided that Gandhi should travel overnight to Nairobi, where, by prior arrangement, our sisal agents gave him fifteen thousand shillings to deliver to us. Twenty-two years later we are still waiting for Gandhi to turn up with our money.

FOUR

'Mind, the poor general was quite brilliant!'

Sher was telling us how a very prominent army general in some European country lost his fame, fortune and family in his blind passion for Mata Hari, the mystic lady whom the French executed as a war spy in 1917. If Sher wanted attentive ears he had them. The story was quite saucy. As became his regular habit, he was wearing a jacket and necktie. Since he had been unable to find a shirt with a collar large enough to cover the whole of his neck the noose of the tie covered only a part of the garment and the rest ran around his bare skin.

Just as we were coming to a very interesting episode, we heard some noises in the driveway. One of the drivers of the tractors which pulled sisal trailers from the estate to the factory was in the compound. He was panting heavily. In between his gasps we got the story. He had a serious problem. He was pulling a fully laden trailer over the main railway line which passed through the middle of the plantation when the towbar snapped. The trailer was stuck smack in the middle of the railway line. He had spent some hours trying to haul it off, and now it was after ten on a very dark night.

'Bwana, the main passenger train is due very shortly to pass the point where my trailer is stuck. I don't want to get into trouble, you will understand.'

The tractor driver's anxiety *was* understandable. I looked at my watch. Not more than fifteen minutes were left to find a solution. One could hardly ring the stationmaster and ask him if he would kindly keep his train hanging around the station for a couple of hours while we went looking for mechanics, gas cylinders etc to clear his line.

We rushed to the scene of impending disaster in Sher's Land-Rover which carried a rope. We tied one end to the trailer and the other end was hooked up to the Land-Rover. As Sher put his vehicle in full power the rope snapped like thin string. A trailer heavily loaded with sisal leaves was not to be towed away that easily. We started a second attempt when the train whistle blew about a mile and a half down the line.

'Let us all hide behind the bush and leave the rest to God,' was Sher's solution.

'Is that the best you can do?' I asked protestingly. But we immediately followed him as the sharp beam of the loco-motive came into sight.

The driver on the footplate of the loco saw the obstruction and gave a quick tug on a cord hanging overhead. The short whistle did not seem to make any effect on whatever was occupying the loco's path. He blew a longer whistle. The object stayed put defiantly. To get the eight hundred ton load going again on a 1.5 per cent gradient would take some doing – and induce a chain of jolts through all coaches where most of the passengers were by then asleep.

He must have lost valuable time in his deliberation because, by the time he pushed down his steam regulator and applied the air pressure brakes, the loco had hit the trailer. The five ton trailer stood not a chance against a two hundred and fifty ton locomotive. It flew into the sky bring-ing down a shower of sisal bundles.

The Sikh loco driver jumped down from his short iron ladder, leaving his fireman in charge of the machine. He had a flash-lamp in one hand and a pipe wrench in the other, to assess the situation. There was hardly a dent on the locomotive and the object of his unscheduled halt was nowhere to be seen. In fact, the trailer was lying in darkness some twenty yards away in the bush – all four wheels in the air.

The driver moved his flash-lamp about to see if he could dig out the truth. Then the beam caught the frightened faces of the tractor driver and his mates who had come out of their hiding place in the bush to avoid the downpour of sisal bundles. Unfortunately, they had run in the wrong direction.

The Sikh loco driver lost his temper. Mtito Andei station was only two hours away, where, at midnight, he would be replaced by a relief driver. Instead of going to sleep he would now have to prepare some sort of report that would have to be presented to the Traffic Controller the next morning in Nairobi.

'Who the bloody hell is responsible for this?' He held his pipe wrench in a threatening manner.

The three of us were still safely hiding behind the bush. 'By God, Sher, he is going to crack open someone's skull,' Rustam whispered.

Sher walked to the scene. We followed.

'It *that* thing yours?' Sher asked Mr Singh, accusingly pointing to the giant locomotive towering above us – smoke belching, steam hissing from a multitude of pipes and joints, and the rumbling, angry inferno in the belly of the firebox lighting up the surrounding area where a small crowd now stood.

The loco driver started to say something but Sher cut him short.

'Did you see what you have done to our precious sisal trailer?' Sher looked questioningly at the loco driver. I said to myself, come on Sher, don't tell a shameless lie, the trailer is due for the scrapyard any day now – every traffic constable in the area wants to pounce on it the minute it comes on the main road outside the plantation.

But Mr. Singh had obviously not expected such an unproportionately huge man to walk out of the darkness of the night. Things will have to be soft pedaled, he must have thought.

'Do you normally park your trailer on the railway lines?' the loco driver shouted back.

Sher simply stared at him. There were some pregnant moments as the two of them faced each other like angry dogs, without saying anything further. Then, very upset, Mr. Singh climbed back to the footplate. He repositioned his reversing gear and pulled up the steam regulator as he released the Westinghouse brake. His obedient giant, *5910 Mount Henang,* trembled from end to end for a moment and then started inching away.

As the end section of the locomotive passed the point where our group stood, the loco driver tilted a small brass lever in his cab. A blast, scorching and scalding, from the steam release valve on the rear cylinder of the loco sent us all running into the bush. Poor Sher could not move fast enough and took a lot of beating. I had better not mention what language he was using as the 'one-up' passed us.

Rustam and I started, with the tractor driver and his people, to collect the strewn sisal bundles, while Sher gazed thoughtfully at the red lamp at the back of the train. When it had finally melted into the darkness he turned round and said:

'Women can be really destructive.'

'Why are you cursing women? That loco driver was a man. Did it escape your notice?' I asked.

'I was thinking of Mata Hari!'

*   *   *

When Rustam and I first arrived, there was another sisal estate called Masinga attached to the main one at Voi. It was about two miles away and smaller in size. It had five thousand acres of good sisal leaves but the sisal processing factory and the infrastructure were in a dilapidated state. The factory machinery was very much out of date. However, it was being sold by its British owners at such a temptingly cheap price that our father and his partner decided to buy it.

To look after this setup of Masinga, our father's partner had recruited a person called Vithaal from India because someone had told him that he was a 'good farmer'. One would be very hard pressed to imagine what kind of Indian farmer would know about a sisal plantation, especially one which was on the fringe of a national park where scores of lions and other wild animals prowled defiantly after dusk. Vithaal was mortified of these animals. No matter what happened, come five o'clock, he would scuttle to his house and lock the gate for the night. Ironically for him, inside the house he had to face quite a violent and dictatorial wife. Thus Vithaal was surrounded by hostilities and had very little in life to give any pleasure.   But the most hostile of all was the Factory Inspector who paid periodic visits. This particular Factory Inspector at that time, Mr. Fairchild, the one with an ancient looking wife, was a whisker short of being a full-blown monster. I can imagine Vithaal concluding his evening prayers with a request to his Maker: "God, I accept this horrible woman of mine. I will also put up with those man-eating lions. But, please God, spare me from that white Satan, the mad factory inspector."

The Factory Inspector would go to Masinga after having inspected our factory of Voi first. By no stretch of imagination would he take our leave without belching out a salvo of verbal abuses and labelling us as being the epitome of everything that was evil in this world!

However, to Vithal he was a nemesis of unimaginable proportion.

"Not even a pig can stay in your labour quarters and survive beyond one month. He would die of some dreadful disease." Fairchild was shouting at Vithal on one particular visit. "And it will remain one of the unsolved mysteries of mankind how and when the workers take their bath in this place."

"Every time it rains." Vithal whispered, almost to himself very softly. But he had underestimated Fairchild's sensitive ears.

"I believe you there." Fairchild cried out loudly.

"We are in process of putting up first class bathrooms. Honestly sir."

"That is what you have been telling me for the past two years, you rotten liar." Short of punching Vithal's nose, Fairchild could not have been more aggressive towards our poor Mr. Vithal.

That night he did not go home. His wife began to be worried and at about nine rang the wife of our field assistant, Sheriff. Sheriff went looking for Vithal. He found him sitting on a large boulder, not far from the factory. He was in an absolutely dejected mood, face buried in his palms.

"What are you doing here?" Sheriff asked him.

"I remembered India."

"You can do that at home. This is not the place to be at night. Do you know that hungry lions keep on moving around in this place?"

"I have faced more ferocious things in my life than man eating lions of Tsavo."

After some persuasion he agreed to go back home.

On the way, he made a request to Sheriff. "Next time that Empire Builder comes around, can you give me a ring, hey Sheriff! God will do very much good to you, honestly, Sheriff."

Sheriff agreed. He delivered Vithal safely to his wife.

Some six months later there was a call to Vithal on the crank-handle telephone. (Such telephones were common in those days.) "There is a loose cannon ball in the district." Sheriff was warning.

"Jesus Christ!" Vithal said, a chill running down his spine.

Then he bolted. He simply bolted.

He sat in the company's Land Rover and burst out at the speed of a bank robber's get-away car. All the workers stopped working and looked at this new development with awe, their jaws dropped. Soon the vehicle disappeared in a great cloud of red dust. In a short while the Factory Inspector was there. "Where is that manager of yours?" he inquired from the clerks in the office. He was told that he had driven off towards the sisal fields.

"Give me one of the field assistants. I want to fish him out."

Fairchild criss-crossed the sisal fields for an hour or so. At last he found Vithal at the far end of the fields, standing by his car in the scorching sun.

"What on earth are you doing here?"

"I am looking at the scenery. Africa looks so beautiful from here, sir!"

"You shameless liar. The temperature is in its upper thirties. You are perspiring and panting like a long distance runner. And you are trying to convince me that you are admiring the scenery in tropical mid-noon? In any event, do you get paid to run a factory or watch the African landscape?'

" I was on my way to the factory, honestly sir."

"All right. Let us drive back to your so called factory."

At the factory Vithal got the worst grilling of his life.

Next time Vithal got a 'loose cannon ball' warning he bolted again. But he wanted to act smart this time. He drove his protesting vehicle to a certain corner of the field where there was a dry and very narrow riverbed. Only a four-wheel vehicle could go past it. Vithal negotiated his Land Rover past it and dug into thick thorny bush. Fairchild's prestigious British model would get stuck if it tried to pass it. The Factory inspector looked for Vithal in every corner of the sisal fields without much success. After two hours he came back to the factory and told the other workers to give a message to that 'small devil' that the next time around he would come with a court order accompanied by a policeman with a pair of handcuffs.

Meanwhile Vithal stayed put. He came home well past midnight. He was shivering and had high temperature.

He was given medicines and was admonished in no uncertain terms by his wife and other well wishers, Sheriff not excluded. He had nothing to say apart from inquiring from time to time:

"Has he gone?"

"Look, you are being very stupid." His wife scolded him.

"Has he gone?"

"For God's sake Vithal, try to be a little more careful." Sheriff advised him.

"Has he gone?"   Vithal had gone into delirium.

Mercifully soon afterwards, this Tom and Jerry show came to an end. It was decided that Masinga Factory was too outdated and worn out to operate economically. It was shut down and the leaves from that area were ferried to Voi for processing.

Vithal took a steerage passage back to India. Some months later his wife wrote a letter of thanks to Sheriff's wife. Casually she mentioned that her husband was fine but if anyone ever as much as mentions the word 'Africa' he begins to get nightmares for weeks on end.

I expect Vithal must have thought for the rest of his life that God had created Africa for the wild animals, devils and Empire Builders only. No man in his right mind should as much as think of that continent.

FIVE

The previous season's rains were not of very much help. In a few months the effects were beginning to wear off. Lush green vegetation in the district turned into mild green and then into pale green. Soon patches of brown began to appear in random places.

'Gathering storms!' Sher commented.

'Where is the storm? We don't see a cloud in the sky,' said Rustam.

'That is just a phrase I borrowed.'

That was true. Ironically, mild sunny weather always preceded the type of 'storm' we were beginning to learn to live with. Less green vegetation around always drew the elephants to evergreen sisal plants. The situation was getting critical on the eastern flank of the plantation, Masinga.

Soon the first elephants infiltrated into the plantation. They ate up a few plants and were back into Tsavo National Park by the morning. Gradually the number of herds paying nocturnal visits increased. Within a matter of weeks the situation had reached a point where the herds that had feasted during the night crossed other elephant groups from the national park on the latter's way to fill their bellies and moisten their throats. They snapped off the middle part of the plant – or 'heart', as it is referred to in planters' language – with their trunks and chewed it up like sugar cane for its moisture.

The park authorities were informed of the situation by Sheriff who carried the messages back and forth.

They said, 'We have a large area to look after. *You* should protect your property.'

We said, 'We cannot go on firing guns in the air and keep blowing off fire crackers like the Fourth of July day and night, week-in, week-out. There are not enough thunder-flashes in the country to confront your animals. We will be bankrupt in a month. You have trained scouts who have the know-how to confine the beasts within your premises. We hate killing elephants as much as you do.'

Before Sheriff paid a visit to the park offices he had been coached thoroughly by us on the case law of *Rayland* versus *Fletcher*. This involved an English common law case covering consequences of nuisance transferring from one's own premises to that of one's neighbour.

'We have never heard of your Mr Rayland nor Mr Fletcher. If you are so desperate to protect your crop we suggest you build a fence along the boundary. Or even dig a trench,' came the reply.

What sort of fence would turn back a mob of hungry and thirsty elephants! And it was one thing to dig a short trench around a lodge in the middle of the park, and quite another to dig one around our boundary, miles and miles long. Ours was a small private company, not a multinational one.

The situation had been made even more difficult by the fact that the usual game warden had been transferred and the newcomer was indifferent to private grievance – perhaps because his volume of work was increasing in the wake of more and more professional hunters coming to our area for trophies.

'One day I am going to go really mad,' Sher commented at this time.

'You mean there is a higher degree of madness?' I said in light humour.

Sher slowly turned his face towards me and looked directly

in my eyes. Normally he would have chuckled at such a comment. This time his eyes carried a different message.

A few days later he did go mad. The whole episode lasted barely twelve hours, but we had never seen Sher behave in such a manner.

Rustam and I were fiddling around with a transmission belt in the brush machine when a baboon guard bicycled from Masinga with a message from our hunter.

'Bwana wants more bullets for his guns,' was the message. Why would Sher need more ammunition? He always carried enough rounds with him.

'Bwana, he is killing elephants. He is killing lots of them,' the baboon guard volunteered. 'And, Bwana, he has told all us guards to get the hell away from Masinga. We might get shot accidentally, he says.'

It was about nine o'clock in the morning. We went to Sher's house and collected more rounds for his two rifles. Driving to Masinga we saw clouds of red dust at different places in the field. The Masinga section of the plantation was sandwiched between the national park on the east and by a road built by the water works to maintain their pipeline on the west.

Having driven along the pipeline road, we stopped at a spot which was on a slightly higher elevation. From there the whole field could be seen. The place was alive with scores of yelling elephants, only they were not in groups. They were scattered all around the place. If one was running in one direction, another was running directly opposite. Each one was in a panic. As they ran, clouds of dust blew from under their thundering feet.

A faint noise of gunshot was heard from the other end of the field. It was followed rapidly by another shot. There was a cry of a dying elephant, just audible from where we were. At least now we knew where Sher was. We drove there taking a longer and safe route. Elephant guns have a fairly long range.

'Give me my bullets and keep out of my way.' Our hunter was trembling and perspiring. He was in no mood for civil talk. Both of us hung around him, not uttering a word. Sher was busy watching which elephant was moving where. A little later he calmed down and decided to talk to us.

'I am no longer going to fold my arms and watch the elephants make mincemeat of these plants, while the game warden preaches over my shoulder "Please do not shoot animals, They are part of our . . ." Look Mwagudu!' He interrupted his sentence, pointing his finger for his gun bearer. 'That one there. It is not far from the pipeline road.' He drove off with Mwagudu.

We were not sure what was actually happening, or what we should do. One truth was emerging. Sher had gone berserk. Something had triggered off the pent up anger and frustration of the past weeks. He had been fairly restricted from hunting. Now, suddenly, the lid seemed to have been blown off. If he had his way he would mow down every elephant within sight.

It was ridiculous for the two of us to sit in the car doing nothing. After a little deliberation we drove hesitantly to where he had gone. By the time we reached him, he had brought down two more beasts. He paid no attention to our presence, as he went on wiping his forehead with the red handkerchief he always carried with him.

Mwagudu was more helpful. He told us how it had all started. They had come to Masinga early in the morning. Driving on the road along the park border they saw about twelve to fifteen herds of elephants making their way deep into the sisal blocks. Sher stopped his Land-Rover and sat rubbing his cheeks with the palms of his hands. For a full ten minutes he watched the animals leisurely plucking 'hearts' from the sisal plants as they moved on. Then he drove closer to the herd that was nearest and shot down its leader. The other members of the family panicked and, instinctively, started running back towards the park. But

Sher was in their way. He brought down one more. Now there was absolute chaos and disorganisation. They started running in the opposite direction to where the pipeline road lay. All this had taken not more than five minutes.

Then Sher moved to the next herd which must have heard the loud bangs, but having been used to the thunder-flash noises of late, did not pay much attention. Once more the family leader was shot down. Once more there was panic and the family was frightened into running away from the direction of the park. Like the first herd they were heading for the pipeline road. There was no time now for the stampeding elephants to pluck the sisal hearts. All they wanted was to get out of firing range of the madman who was shooting at them. Plants and bushes which were in their way were trampled on and uprooted. Sher had caught up with five herds before the rest of them realised that this was no empty threat. Their leaders hurriedly guided them back into the sanctuary of the game park.

As the confused members of the latest victimised family reached the vicinity of the pipeline road, Sher was waiting for them. He had quickly driven across the field and was running up and down the road. Mwagudu, meanwhile, had been continuously loading and reloading his rifle. Sher started dropping more elephants, as they made an about turn and headed back to where they had come from. And there, Sher's car was waiting once more, the hunter having driven back to his starting place.

Some elephants had managed to run back into the park. Some had crossed the pipeline road, crossed the railway line, and the Nairobi-Mombasa Road, and were now heading for far horizons. Some were running in the direction of the Indian Ocean. Anywhere but here. All of them were not lucky. There were quite a number of them still trapped in between.

'Too much blood is being spilt,' Mwagudu whispered to us in protest as he concluded his story.

'Sher, don't you think that is enough?' we ventured. But he took no notice of our presence. He continued drinking water from his canvas flask while his eyes searched for more targets.

It was fully one minute before he came closer to Mwagudu and picked out one of the guns the tracker was carrying. We expected one more shot, one more dead elephant. Instead, he fired into the air.

'Damn you who shout loudest about wildlife preservation without bringing in some sense of proportion. I wish you would join with us in planting sisal as our skins burn under scorching sun. I wish you would wait with us for occasional rain to see the plants grow up. And, finally, when the sisal is ready after four years, watch with us these animals destroy the hearts of it. Perhaps you would sing a different tune then. What happened to your own wild buffalo and bison? You slaughtered them in thousands, didn't you, to make room for your wheat fields? Very convenient talking about heritage for the future, as long as this is not happening in your own country? You double . . .' His last words were lost in yet another loud explosion from his elephant gun. He was shaking with rage.

Hunting vehicles normally carry a first aid box. A quarter bottle of brandy was extracted from it and handed to him. He gulped down every drop of it and slumped over the steering wheel, head resting on the rim. A solitary tear rolled down his rotund cheek.

Everyone needs to be left alone at times. For Sher this was the time to be left alone and we silently withdrew. Rustam went back to our car and lit his cigarette. Mwagudu sat on the ground with his back resting on the rear wheel of the Land-Rover while he went through the motions of emptying rifle magazines and rearranging hunting gear. I walked about a hundred yards away and sat on a small anthill.

Everything was now quiet on that November Saturday

afternoon. All remaining elephants had disappeared. The dust had settled. On the horizon lay lonely Yatta Plateau. Silence was occasionally interrupted by wind sweeping over this part of the Taru Desert. It seemed as if the four of us were the only occupants of the planet. At random spots lay the remains of the casualties.

Thirteen of them.

That evening Rustam and I decided to pay a call at Sher's house. He was seated on a safari chair that had been put out in the garden under a jacaranda tree. On the table next to him was a primitive model of a gramophone which was playing some European classical symphony. I had not seen the contraption before. It must have been retrieved from the store behind the house where he kept charcoal, since the thing was full of black particles. Also on the table was a bottle of Red Label and a jug of water. He was sipping his drink slowly from a tin mug. No crystal glasses and ice buckets for this man of the bush. He was oblivious of our arrival. We sat on the chairs that his house servant brought out when he saw us arriving, one on either side of Sher. He seemed to be gazing blankly at a distant horizon. Perhaps he was not gazing his eyes simply open while he was thinking of something else. Perhaps his mind was even blank.

The three of us sat quietly, and the house servant brought tea. It was an idiotic scene three of us with somber faces as if we had just come back from burying a very close friend. The gramophone record came to the end of the symphony. Sher put his mug on the table and wound up the machine. The same symphony came back to life again. Sher picked up his mug and spoke:

'The Queen should remember me in her Birthday Honours list. Twenty blooming elephant!' His speech was slurred. Evidently he had been liberal with the whisky.

'Not twenty. There were thirteen,' he was corrected.

He seemed unconcerned about the discrepancy in the number of animals shot and went on sipping from his tin mug, gazing blankly into the distance. The symphony was on its fourth round when Rustam decided to break the silence.

'You seem to be feeling guilty about killing the animals. Listen to me, Sher. Some day go to a coffee farm in the Thika area. Watch as the spraying machine passes through rows of coffee trees. You will notice clouds of deadly chemicals engulfing the plants. Millions of tiny insects and pests fall to the ground. Most of them are dead even before they hit the ground.' Rustam paused to see if Sher was registering what was being said to him. 'And yet each insect has a soul, the same way a man has, or a dog has, or an elephant has.' Rustam was trying to drive his point home. 'Each has an equal instinct of self preservation,' Rustam concluded.

'But they don't cry and spout blood as the seventeen elephants did today.' Sher had been listening after all.

'Thirteen,' I corrected again.

'And also take the example of the last war.' Rustam was trying to draw another parallel. 'Do you know how many millions of human beings lost their lives? Humans like you and me. And what was the cause of all that carnage? Nobody's farms or businesses or industries were under threat. It all began when one megalomaniac decided that the country he was ruling was too small for his ego. He ordered his army to march across and possess one neighbouring country, and then another. The rest is history.'

'Don't you give me anything about the last war. I know everything. That swine Montgomery wanting to chop the poor British people into tiny pieces. Horrible he was.'

'No. It was Hitler. Montgomery was a British field marshall. He was a good guy.' I tried to correct him once again.

'What difference does a name make? There is always somebody wanting to kill somebody. That is why I feel so awful. Those elephants were crying as I shot them. And there was all that blood around . . . and yet I went on shooting them. And they cried even louder. I had a gun and they did not. Those elephants cursed me as they, died. And as they fell their eyes cursed me while they lay in that twilight zone between life and death. But they were bad. They were eating those sisal plants. Have you ever seen a sisal plant? I mean you must have, since . . .'

Sher's pronouncements were going round and round. He was thoroughly mixed up and very, very drunk. We decided it was time to leave. As we prepared to go he asked me:

'How many elephants did you say I shot today?'

During the night Sheriff, the field officer, supervised a gang of about forty workers to remove the tusks from the dead elephants. By 9.00 a.m. they had been ferried to the factory compound. There turned out to be twenty-five tusks instead of twenty-six. One of the males might have lost one in pursuit of an amorous adventure. Each tusk was weighed, labelled and entered in the game trophy book. They were to be delivered to the local game department who would, in turn, auction them. The proceeds would go to the country's treasury.

When Sher arrived he had regained his composure and was himself once again. Our hunter was clean-shaven and dressed in a neat and freshly pressed pair of khaki trousers and shirt. Anyone within six yards of him could smell the aftershave lotion. On one shoulder was slung his large cannon-like Express 600 elephant rifle.

'I have every intention of delivering Her Majesty's belongings to her storekeeper in person – and on foot.' We tried to dissuade him, but he would not have it.

He led the caravan in the olden-day ivory trader single-file manner. Mwagudu walked alongside Sher, and twenty-five of the baboon guards followed them, each with one tusk slung over his shoulder. Starting from the factory compound they crossed the railway line, went down the dusty road through to the market, passed the trading centre, up to the District Officer's headquarters, (where the DO stepped out of his office, momentarily chewing his pencil to witness with dismay yet one more act of lunacy) and down the valley to the office of the game department – a total distance of about two miles. The route was thronged with curious onlookers. Most of them were village urchins. Some waved to the procession; some joined the tail end; and yet others preferred to throw tiny stones at them.

The game warden and his staff were aware of the previous day's shootings. They were expecting the ivory to be delivered – but not in this fashion. There was nothing in their game law as to how animal trophies should be delivered, so there was nothing upon which they could comment. Sher took no notice of their twisted faces.

'Here are the tusks of the elephants that were shot during control work, Sir.' Sher was being official. Normally the word *Sir* did not exist in his vocabulary, especially when talking to the officials of game or park departments.

'May we have your signature here, please, Sir?' Sher handed over his delivery book.

The message had finally shot home to the park authorities. Within twenty-four hours scores of game scouts were placed along the common border of the park and plantation. Tents were pitched, a vehicle was seen running up and down the plantation boundary, and some walkie-talkies were also deployed.

All this was not necessary. The stench of the dead animals kept the rest away from the area for months on end.

Chacha (FAR LEFT), Rustam (FAR RIGHT) with Gina Lollobrigida at Chacha's camp in the early seventies.

ABOVE: The house on the hill through whose front doors walked all ranks of people from a prince, later to become king of England, to a pauper, who died penniless on the streets of Nairobi.   BELOW: Mzee Mwagudu.

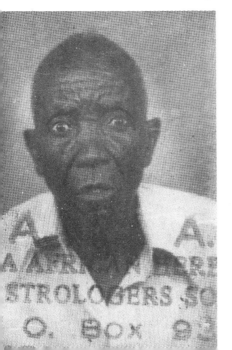

ABOVE: Sher with a dead elephant. (Author behind him)
BELOW: Sher's tusk caravan.

AUTHOR and his family with the Layzell daughters and their friends on the front steps of the house. The late Major Layzell was manager of the plantation in the thirties. In 19 two of the daughters, Catherine – the late Lady Lloyd (BOTTOM LEFT) and Anne (RIG OPPOSITE HER) – accompanied their mother, Margaret, when she drove Karen Blixen friend, Denys Finch-Hatton, to Voi Airstrip on the fringe of the plantation. They saw h take off in his small 'plane and witnessed with horror as it fell into the plains.

(Picture taken by Mr. Edward Rodwell in 1974)

SIX

'Well, I have told you the reason,' Sher said. He had suddenly and unexpectedly decided to resign from the company.

Sher and Rustam were sitting under the jacaranda tree at the former's house. Earlier in the day he had asked if Rustam could come to his house and have tea with him in the evening. I was in bed with a touch of flu.

'I have come across many reasons for someone to give up a job,' Rustam said to Sher. 'People have left the company because either there were not enough school facilities for their children, or the climate did not agree with them, or there was better opportunity elsewhere. But your decision to leave Voi and look for a job in Nairobi takes the cake. One does not just resign because one does not get the opportunity to dress up in a jacket and tie.'

Sher remained quiet and rubbed his cheeks with his palms, as was his habit when in thoughtful mood.

'All right then, please do wear your tie and your jacket. I will not say anything to that. The company will even buy you whatever you want to wear.'

'But my job here is as a hunter!'

'Then go hunting wearing clothes of your choice.'

'And make a complete ass of myself? If you had your way you might suggest that I buy a bowler hat and an umbrella for good measure.' Sher tried to put across his extraordinary reasoning. 'You have missed the point altogether. Say, if in Nairobi I dress the way I want, and then go meter reading for the water department, no one would so much as raise an eyebrow.'

It usually pays not to stand in the way of a man in pursuit of his fancy. But it was sad to see Sher leaving for such an unaccountable reason as dressing in a jacket and tie.

We accompanied Sher to the railway station the night he was leaving for Nairobi. Even as he pushed his slightly bulging old suitcase under the berth of his compartment, he decided to enlighten us a little more upon historical facts.

'Eva Peron's death in 1952 was actually faked.'

Here we go again, I said to myself. By now we knew him well enough to judge what to believe and what to discard. This time he was prepared to swear that he had read these facts of Argentinian history in a highly reputable American magazine which specialised in digging into historical truths and myths. 'Her president husband's colleagues were getting somewhat restless about the power the lady was wielding through the country's radio network. She may have been friends of the shirtless, but she was no friend of her husband's close advisers. The president had to yield to the pressure and the only plausible way of removing her from the political scene was to fake her death.'

Sher had not finished his version when the train began to move:

'She is still alive and well and stays high up in the Andes at a place called . . . damn . . . gramophone . . . is . . .'

The distance between us and the coach carrying our hunter had lengthened, so his last words were barely audible.

'I do not understand this. What could Eva Peron have to do with a gramophone?' I asked Rustam.

'I think he was trying to say that he has left his gramophone behind.'

Sher had been gone about three months when there was

some loud knocking at the front door early one morning. I looked at my watch: five o'clock. I picked up the kerosene lamp and came out of the house rubbing my eyes. It was the watchman who had knocked on the door. Next to him stood a boy about twelve years old.

'Mwagudu has sent fifty cents with this boy. He wants to buy a pint of milk,' the watchman said. 'The boy says Mwagudu is very sick. He says he needs milk to regain his strength.' I was still rubbing my eyes and trying to make some sense of all this business of Mwagudu, milk and money. It took a few moments before I realized that it was Mwagudu who was sick. He must be very sick, I thought. He was not a person to press the panic button quickly.

We took some milk and walked to Mwagudu's small hut which was not very far. I stepped inside and took a look at our tracker. He was very sick indeed. He had evidently gone through a period of diarrhea and vomiting during the night. There was no strength left in him, even to move his arms or to tell us how it happened or when it all began. One did not have to be a doctor to tell that the man was dying of dehydration.

Mwagudu, were you trying to bargain your life with fifty cents worth of milk at this stage? Your body needed gallons of water and maybe countless pints of blood. Not fifty cents worth of milk!
He was quickly removed to the hospital. Doctors started working on him. A saline drip-needle was pushed into his vein. Blood was transfused. All that was necessary was done.

It was mid-day when Mwagudu passed away.

So you have to depart from the scene, Mwagudu. But

that is part of the process called life. You could not have chosen your fate as much as I cannot choose mine. At times I imagine us all as fellow passengers going back home on a suburban city train after the day's work. We meet and discuss the weather, or families and various topics. One after another we step down at our respective stations. Your station came earlier. However, like most of us small insignificant beings of this world, your passing away will hardly make any dent, except to your immediate family and the few of us whose lives were intertwined, both because of our common aims as well as for liking and understanding each other.

The world at large will hardly know your worth. With your soul you carried away your wisdom. You knew when to send your woman to the field with a hoe to prepare the land in time for the rains – whether Sher sent his balloons up or not. You made no complaints to anyone when you had to cut down on weekly rations so the school fees could be paid for your child. You always kept spare grass handy so that when the rains came the roof of your hut was properly thatched. All these domestic competencies were born out of tolerance and existential needs. Simplicity was the keyword in your life. You found more joy in your old Roamer wrist-watch than others have in their Mercs. The world will forget you when the cycle comes to its end. No one will erect a monument in your memory, Mwagudu.

Neither will a monument be erected in recognition of your professional ability. No – but not because you were not good enough.

I am thinking of a past great hunter in our own country.* He was white and came from an aristocratic background. Princes and presidents took him along on their hunting safaris. He knew what to talk about to them, and how to eat with them. You did not know all these things, did you Mwagudu? You were born at a different time in a different

*Denys Finch-Hatton

country and your mind was much too simple to understand their protocol. There was even this factor of biological differences, the cause of a great number of human sufferings.

I am told that this white hunter was very good in his profession and that is why the dignitaries took him along when hunting. Not because he had a noble background – there were lots of them around then – but because he was a good hunter.

It is not out of the blue that I am bringing him into my thoughts at this moment. His fate, too, was to a certain extent, interwoven with Voi. He was a frequent visitor to Major Lazell, when the latter was the manager of the plantation in the thirties. In fact, he spent his very last night alive in this huge house where Rustam and I were presently staying.

Next morning his small airplane betrayed him in failing to develop enough power to lift him and his servant into the sky at a critical moment. They dropped into the plains and died – yes the very same plains where Sher and you, Mwagudu, used to move around during control works. A monument has been erected in his memory, where his girlfriend's farm was. Then this lady left the country – never to come back again.*

But you cannot have been less when it came to shooting wild game. I am saying this, although I have not seen this other hunter in action. He died before I was even born, so I have seen only one side of the coin. I seem to sound biased when bringing this comparison. I am not subtracting any point from him. I am only trying to add points for you, even if it is a hopeless effort.

I will never forget the day when Sher's gun got jammed. You were standing next to him holding his other gun as the angry buffalo charged. Some distance away I was sitting in the Land-Rover trembling in my boots.

*Baroness Karen Blixen authoress of *Out of Africa*, among other books.

You lifted the gun in your hand. This was no ordinary situation where the hunter has all the time in the world to study his unsuspecting target and take aim. You were calm, yet quick and swift in removing the safety catch, taking aim and pulling the trigger that sent the bullet into the animal with the precision of a surgeon's knife.

I could not help throwing up as the brains of the creature blew out through both ears. You stood as cool as a block of ice.

My very personal assessment is that you, and your type, maybe in other professions, too, like those of a farmer or cobbler, or those of a sugarcane or sisal cutter, who have made our country what it is today. Not the ones whose first 'cold one' commences at ten in the morning. Nor the ones who throng the nightspots well past midnight. Their end of the month pay-packet would be coming all the same.

You are in no need of any specific monument, Mwagudu. Some of us who lived and watched you at close range understand: this very country is a monument to you and your like.

Let one find Mzee Mwagudu and he has found Kenya.

Yes, Mwagudu was there then, I said to myself as I got up from the concrete culvert I was sitting on at Bachuma Station. I was engrossed in your question: *'Do you still remember what it was like at Voi in those days?'*

Surprisingly not a single train had passed during all that time. There was a fresh easterly wind blowing over the Taru Plains. On the western horizon the sinking sun was screened off by amber clouds. Probably my car had been repaired. But I was in no hurry.

Yes, Mwagudu was there and so was Sher, I thought as once more I sat down on the cement culvert and reverted to my recollection of Voi of those days

76

A few years later, I bumped into an old acquaintance on Christmas Eve in a Nairobi hotel. We indulged in small talk and as he was leaving he casually said. 'I forgot to mention. Since Sher once worked with you, you would like to know that he died a few days back.........,' The rest of his words were lost to me. I slumped into the nearest chair. All I could see was that the crowd around me was dancing and singing and drinking wine. I said to myself that why should it matter to them if Sher has died or not! When their and my time comes we will go while some others will be dancing and merry making. The show goes on, they say.

Yes, Sher and Mwagudu are dead and gone. But they were with us at Voi, I remember.......

But then there were others too......

SEVEN

'Will you please excuse me! It is late. I have to attend a church service.'

Rustam and I were having a friendly talk with the new security officer who had come to replace Sher. The new man was clean-shaven and neatly dressed. He looked plain and simple and someone not given easily to talk. He was a family man. His wife and son had moved in with him. A man who is so concerned about punctuality for religious ceremonies cannot be an unreliable person. That was our initial impression of Mr Adam.

As one grows older life teaches us lessons – and the older one grows the more one knows. Until a stage when, if one happens to grow too old, one is so mixed up with 'facts', 'half-facts' and 'contradictory facts' that the mind is confused. Younger people call this condition 'senile'.

At our stage we were just beginning to learn some unexpected truths. In the next few months I was to find out how much influence the devil has on nature's creations. Nature gave to the earth the beautiful rose. The devil put thorns on the rose bush. Nature sent a pretty woman. The devil saw that behind that beautiful face lay a mind that could ruin lives. Nature thought of delicious grapes. The devil was quick to ferment the fruit into alcohol.

Generally, everything the world has, the devil has made sure to have a little of his influence in it. Everyone, too, has a little bit of the devil in him. However, normally good and bad run simultaneously in nature's creations. Rarely does one come across someone who is saintly for weeks on end only to lie hopelessly possessed by some uncontrollable evil influence for the next few days. Adam was to teach us a thing or two about human nature . . .

Musa, the baboon guard, was more asleep than awake under a shady tree when the rogue rhino charged, so he never knew what happened. It was instant death.

The new security officer was sent for to track the culprit and shoot it down. A rhino is normally a harmless creature. He does not eat or trample sisal. But if he should be mixed up with a gang of sisal cutters the resulting situation could be very unpleasant.

Adam walked into the office. He was staggering more than walking and he could hardly keep his eyes open. Evidently he had not shaved for some days. He was not the man we had seen a few weeks back.

'What do you want?' he shouted at me. I was surprised at the change in this person. The circumstances were explained to him. He kept his eyes closed while listening to Rustam.

'I will go and get my guns,' was his reply as he strode off.

He and his trackers and gun bearers went rhino tracking The animal was not found on the first day, nor the next. However, it was still within the sisal fields, since some of the sisal cutters had seen him wandering around. On the third day we decided to join Adam. It was a Sunday and we did not have anything better to do. The three of us sat in the front of the Land-Rover while his trackers and gun bearers sat in the back. Adam still looked and behaved the way he had done a couple of days back. He spoke very little and whatever he said was difficult to understand. Generally, he gave a picture as if too much fuss was being created about one single rhino. Why waste so much petrol and time over one animal.

Adam was the first to sight the quarry. He stopped the car and walked out with one of the guns. He had walked some yards when I realised that the rhino had noticed us also. The animal neither tried to run away nor to charge our party. Instead he walked to the car with thumping feet. Adam stood out in the open a few yards away from the vehicle, not in the least concerned. The rhino put his horns under the front bumper and shook his head furiously. The car shook up, down and sideways.

One has to learn about fright some day or the other. I regretted accompanying Adam. I wished I had never let Rustam engage him as a security officer. I lamented over coming to Voi. I even cursed Mr Pinto of the Dak Bungalow for talking to my father about sisal. In all this confusion I could not see Adam. I also suddenly realised that the people at the back of the vehicle had mysteriously disappeared into thin air, while the two of us were being jostled around in the cabin. I felt as if the entire human race had deserted us, leaving us two and the stupid rhino as the only occupants of this earth.

The rhino disengaged his horns from under the bumper and started running away slowly. In all likelihood he wanted to go away a few paces then turn around and charge at the vehicle.

He had hardly gone a couple of yards when a shot rang out. Adam had shot the rhino dead. Life had been paid for by life. For the first time in those sixty seconds I saw our hunter. He was yawning and seemed totally bored. Suddenly his gun bearers and trackers began to appear on the scene out of the blue. They had possessed the wisdom of climbing up the nearest tree in sight, we were to learn later.

'Can we all bloody well go home now?' Adam asked Rustam. We all drove back in silence.

When we saw Adam the next day he looked clean and

neat. His speech was soft and polite. The angel in him was back in control. In time to come there was one thing we learnt about him: he was an excellent shot.

Excellent shot or not, angelic or devilish, we never rode with him during control work again. There were better things to do on Sundays than be pushed around by a killer rhino.

A few days later we were to have another taste of his nature.

Park Inn was a popular rendezvous for the small community in Voi. 'Bob' Foster was one of the regular customers. Since resigning from the sisal plantation when we took over, he had been hunting elephant. He never shot one with a weight less than two hundred pounds between the pair of tusks. He had also built a small but comfortable wooden house just on the fringe of the sisal plantation. He was spending his retired life as he had always wanted to spend it. The Game Department had made him an honorary game warden (such honorary wardens rendered sterling service, being watchful on poaching and other irregularities in hunting areas), and he was a person well respected in the district.

At Park Inn Bob Foster saw a new face, our Mr Adam, who had gone in for his couple of pints. In a small place it does not take long to get acquainted with each other, especially for those of common profession. Soon they were offering each other beers and talking of their past experiences.

'Your Mr Adam seems to be a nice person,' Mr Foster made a casual remark to Rustam during one of his routine visits to our office. I thought of telling Mr Foster to be on the lookout when Adam was in his 'mad mood'. Somehow I refrained from making any comment and Mr Foster was to find out for himself a few days later.

He had inspected Masinga area on a casual round one morning. As was common in those days he found a giraffe helplessly trying to untangle a long foot caught in a poacher's snare. That foot was in a bloody mess. The only thing to do under such circumstances was to put the animal to 'sleep'. Mr Foster had done just that and was now on his way to the Game Department to report the incident. Coming out of the estate he had driven along the pipeline road to reach the main road. He recognised the company's Land-Rover coming from the opposite direction and stopped his vehicle to talk to Adam about the giraffe. Adam had also stopped about thirty yards away and Mr Foster started to walk towards him when Adam fired his rifle into the air right over Mr Foster's head.

'You have got to be careful with that . . .' Mr Foster began to say.

This time Adam fired at the ground well past where Mr Foster stood. It was not the time to stand casually by while bullets zoomed past, and Mr Foster turned back.

'Who gave you permission to enter private land?' Adam was shouting at Mr Foster as he handed his gun back to the frightened gun bearer in his Land-Rover.

'Look, Adam, you must have gone crazy. You do not go slaughtering people for a trivial reason like that! Do you know I am an honorary game warden here? Do you know that what you have done could land you into a hell of a lot of trouble with the police?'

'I don't care who you are. Next time you want to enter the company's land you ask my permission. I am the security officer here. You understand that, Mr Foster!'

Mr Foster was certainly in no mood to talk to this man. He jumped into his Land-Rover and drove away. Initially he probably had it in mind to go to the police station. Perhaps during the drive to the village he changed his mind. He had had a very cordial relationship with the company for many years and did not want to get us involved in a scandal. One thing he was very perplexed about: how could a person – just two days back, discussing with him crocodile of the

Tana, bull elephant in the Rufiji region of Tanganyika and white rhino of the West Nile District at a far flung corner of Uganda – suddenly decide to gun him down! The man must be schizophrenic was Mr Foster's conclusion. He came instead to our office.

'I have come to see you about your damn Mr Adam.' Mr Foster was perspiring.

'Why, has he been shouting at you, Mr Foster?'

'No, he has not been shouting at me. He has been S-H-O-O-T-I-N-G at me!' And he narrated the entire incident.

By now we knew that Mr Adam could alter his moods like a chameleon can change colour, but this was the limit. Both of us were extremely upset and did not know how to apologise to Mr Foster adequately. Mr Foster was older and wiser, and promised that he would not refer to the matter any further.

'You be very careful about this man. He will land you in trouble some day,' he warned us before leaving the office, shaking his head in disbelief.

We went looking for Adam. He was not in the Masinga area. We looked for him fruitlessly for hours. When he came back to the factory we were told that he had locked his guns in his house, had dropped his gun bearers and tracker, and had driven off.

Nobody saw Adam for the next two days, not even his family. Finally, when he reappeared on the third day he was again clean-shaven and neatly dressed, as sober as a village padre. Not once did he lift his eyes from the ground as we gave him a piece of our mind. He listened to everything timidly. He made no comment when he was told that from then on he should keep his guns locked in the safe until such time as the company had decided what to do with him. He walked out of the office without saying a word.

In the evening Rustam made a comment to me: 'I am not sure what is more difficult to control, a marauding animal or a mad hunter.' Such incidents do not remain quiet in a small town. Soon the story got round. Adam was not liked by many people. No one ever offered to buy him a beer at the Park Inn from then on.

One evening we came home as tired as we could be. Everything that could go wrong in the factory had gone wrong. On top of all these problems a tractor driver towing a trailer-load of sisal bundles to the factory had sighted a duiker and decided to chase it with his machine. He was hardly in the mood to pay attention to the loud shouts of protest from the four very frightened loaders sitting atop sisal bundles on the trailer. One of them jumped off, fortunately avoiding any injury. (He later on collected his belongings from the labour camp and disappeared from the job without even bothering to take the balance of his salary.)

The other loaders were not so lucky. The machine went zigzagging behind the tiny buck amidst shouts that changed from protests to obscenities. Eventually the machines and men all landed in a deep ravine. There were quite a few broken bones.

Thus, when we came home, all we wanted was to eat our food and hit the hay. As we were dining the telephone rang. Rustam picked it up. He kept on listening with occasional replies of, 'that is right', 'absolutely true', 'no, sir!', 'very well sir!'

When he had finished the call he told me:

'Forget your food. We are wanted at the police station.'

'Oh no! What now?' I was disgusted.

'Superintendent Hopkins is complaining that Adam wants to massacre his entire police force.'

Trouble had started brewing up earlier in the evening.

Adam was driving back from the Park Inn, a little high on spirits and downright low on reasoning. Going down the road near the market he did not notice the police Land-Rover parked on the roadside. It was late in the evening and quite dark. Inside sat a constable and the driver. It was a routine patrol. Adam with half closed eyes ran squarely into the back of the police van. There was a loud crashing noise and the two occupants of the police vehicle quickly came out to investigate what had hit them. Adam had not been driving very fast so no one was hurt. His drooping eyes were now wide open.

Adam's anger was building up: why in God's name cannot some people park properly! He reversed his vehicle for about thirty feet. Then he drove it once again straight into the police van. The constable and his driver ran into the nearby bush. They watched in utter bewilderment as Adam rammed their vehicle three more times. The company's Land-Rover lost the front bumper, radiator, fan, and half the timing chain cover. The police vehicle was in an even worse shape.

By now Adam's anger was spent, or maybe he realised his vehicle was no longer in a shape to do more bullfighting. He started driving towards his house. About half a mile further on our battered Land-Rover stalled, as if in protest at this unwarranted punishment. Adam abandoned it and walked the remaining distance to his house. Then he jumped into bed and fell asleep.

The constable and the driver of the police vehicle hurriedly walked back to the police station. They had recognised the occupant of the company's Land-Rover, and Superintendent Hopkins was in a rage when the incident was narrated. He got a senior inspector and about seven other policemen to pick up Adam while he sat down to think of the number of charges that could be brought against this man. Driving under the influence of alcohol will certainly be one of them, Mr Hopkins thought.

The police party reached Adam's house. They knocked on the door. The house was in complete darkness.

'Who is it?' Adam woke up from a deep slumber.

'Open the door! Superintendent Hopkins wants to see you at the station.'

There was a momentary silence as the policemen waited

for the door to open. The occupant of the house switched on the garden lights. From a window he could see the police party waiting outside. Inside the house it was still dark so Adam had the advantage, and the policemen were unable to see what he was doing. Suddenly a wooden window on the side of the house was flung open. Adam pushed his rifle through the window and fired into the air. He emptied his other barrel for good measure. Insult was added to injury.

The inspector took his party back to the police station. Now, on top of Hopkins's list of charges against Adam, there was an added item: Attempted Murder.

It was at this juncture that we were requested to present ourselves at the police station. After having heard the story we understood why Hopkins was raving mad.

'I have every mind to arm my people and instruct them to shoot their way into your hunter's house. I want him brought here wearing handcuffs, and to have him locked up until the charge sheet has been prepared.'

'You will be justified in doing so, Mr Hopkins.'

'He can go in for a long stretch. This is no longer the intimate little village it used to be when I first came here. These days there is not much time for individual concerns. Have you seen our vehicle? It was a long wheelbase Land-Rover. Thanks to your hunter it has now been squeezed down to a size smaller than a short wheelbase model.'

'Very unfortunate, Mr Hopkins.'

'I have more and more people to look after. The district is growing.'

'That is true, Mr Hopkins.'

'Damn it, don't go on making consenting remarks to whatever I say.' Now he was angry with *us*. He lit his pipe and took a deep puff. We sat opposite him, looking like culprits whose dog had bitten his policemen.

After a pause Hopkins started again: 'I don't want shoot-outs. I don't want any blood. There is, however, one thing I do want and this is where you both come in. You must go personally to persuade your hunter to accompany you to the police station. Also ask him to hand over his gun to an officer whom I will send with you.

I sat on a bench facing the counter of the duty officer, while Rustam drove to Adam's house with a police officer.

'Adam, will you let me in?' Rustam shouted from a safe distance in Adam's garden. Fortunately, Adam recognized the voice and opened the door. Rustam walked in, leaving the policeman in the car.

'What have you been doing, Adam? Of all the millions of people in the world, why did you choose the police as the target on which to aim your tantrums?'

'Look, these policemen at Voi are being a nuisance to the public. Earlier on in the evening they planted their van directly in my way. Fortunately, I did not break my bones. Now they have sent the whole police force to arrest me. Can a man not live in peace! I tell you they are a useless lot.'

'Adam, sit down and let us talk about how to sort out this problem.' After about twenty minutes persuasion he agreed to come to the police station. He also handed his gun over to the police officer.

Inside the superintendent's office he stood yawning widely as Hopkins mentioned the charges under which he could be prosecuted. Attempted Murder; Obstructing a Police Officer from Performing his Duty; Driving Under the Influence of Alcohol; Causing Malicious Damage to Government Property; Resisting Lawful Arrest......the entire Penal Code was here. About the only charge that was not included was that of Piracy on the High Seas.

Adam looked at the ground. There was a pause before he spoke.

'I was not drunk.'

'You have the cheek to say that?'

'Yes, sir.'

'Very well, we will get that fact established before it is too late. Let us walk to the hall.'

At the back of the police station was a hall which was mainly used for minor social events as well as being the police canteen. We all walked to the hall. Across the floor was a straight oil-painted white line. The only doctor in the village was summoned. The state of intoxication had to be established by a medical practitioner.

'Now let us see you walk along that line without staggering,' Hopkins ordered Adam.

Adam walked casually along the line without the slightest sign of faltering. At the far end he turned around and walked back with equal ease. There was pin-drop silenced in the hall. Hopkins was not satisfied.

'Let me see how you can hop along the line on one leg.' Adam hopped along the line flawlessly. At the far end he made an about turn, still on one leg. Then he bowed to the crowd watching him. He hopped back along the white line, smiling all the way, as if amusing a bunch of kids. Somebody in the hall coughed embarrassedly.

'You see, I am not drunk,' Adam said to Hopkins. 'I bet the doctor here can't do what I am subjected to.'

'Don't be silly!' Hopkins had reason to be frustrated. 'The doctor can very well perform such acts. It is no positive test for intoxication.'

'I want to see that,' Adam challenged politely. Hopkins stared at Adam in anger. Then, without shifting his angry eyes from Adam's face he said, 'Doctor, show this man.'

The doctor hopped three paces. Then he fell flat on his back. He was much too plastered to perform such acrobatics.

'I will be damned if I allow this man to get away just like that. Doctor, take his urine sample and have it analysed tomorrow.' Hopkins did not want to give in so easily.

One of the policemen produced an empty bottle and handed it to the doctor. The doctor then led Adam to the toilet, gave him the bottle and stood outside the door. The entire crowd waited for Adam to come out with incriminating evidence. Seconds started ticking and minutes dragging. When Adam had not come out after five or six minutes Hopkins shouted:

'What do you think you are doing in there? We are not going to wait for you until doomsday.'

The toilet door opened and Adam came out holding the bottle in his outstretched hand. It was dry and empty.

'If it isn't there, it isn't there. I am not like those mystics of India who can perform miracles! Maybe if you wait an hour or so there is a chance . . .'

'Shut up. Please shut up. In the name of our Lord Jesus Christ, I beg you to shut up. If you speak so much as one more word I will throttle you.' One could notice that Hopkins was both fed up and tired. He wanted to forget all this. 'Come to my office,' he added.

Back in his office, Hopkins said, 'I think you are more of a clown than a criminal. If I send you for a long trial you are capable of converting a courthouse into a circus. I am dropping all charges except one. You will answer for Maliciously Damaging Government Property. You will sign a bond and appear in court on Monday.'

The superintendent was now more than fed up with this man but Adam got away with a comparatively light fine. Of course, Rustam knew and I knew why Hopkins was lenient over preferring the charges. He was due to retire in two weeks' time and sail back to England. He had a house in the Lake District, he had once told us. Bringing serious charges would have meant court attendances for weeks on end. No, that was not the reason. Hopkins was a very kind-hearted person. Despite what he said at the police station he was very much concerned about every individual he knew. Underneath his 'cop' uniform lay a very tender personality. Although he knew what Adam did was not pleasant by any stretch of the imagination.

Technically Hopkins had not performed his duty 'without fear or favour'. But humans are not machines which function strictly on technicalities. He wanted to leave Kenya with mellow memories of the country and the people. There are many people who want to remember Africa positively, and Assistant Superintendent of Police, John Hopkins, was no exception.

EIGHT

'We have an African cowboy on our hands. The man is plain trigger happy. First poor Mr Foster. Now Hopkins's policeman. I wonder who will be next? How long are we going to put up with him?'

'I wish I knew,' Rustam replied, as he sipped his tea on the verandah. In the evening there was plenty of time to think of our Mr Adam and anticipate with dread what he was likely to do next. During office hours there were routine matters pertaining to sisal production, so not much thought was spared for Mr Adam then.

One day we had a problem with the main diesel engine which ran the decorticator. The cylinder head developed a minor crack and during the night water had dripped into the cylinder. In the morning when Lofty opened the air pressure valve to put the huge flywheel in motion before switching onto diesel, the piston, weighing about half a ton, hit a solid column of water. There was a loud 'thud' and the crankshaft was in two pieces. That was the end of the line for the huge twin cylinder Ruston engine. The engine was a very old model and there were no spares for such machines in the country. An electric motor was bought to run the decorticator. That left the enormous old engine occupying too much valuable space. The whole engine room could be converted into a store if the Ruston engine was removed. But who would do the removal of these large chunks of iron?

Word was passed to some friends in Nairobi and Mombasa as to whether there was any taker for this engine. Soon a scrap dealer called on us. We asked five thousand shillings for the entire machine. He paid a deposit of two thousand shillings and said he would come back with his mechanics and equipment. They all worked for three days but did not get as far as dislodging the huge flywheel. One night they all disappeared.

There was another man who was interested in collecting vintage machines. He took one look at the engine and walked away without so much as saying 'goodbye'. The third buyer was again a scrap dealer. He was more persistent. He and his workers struggled for six days and dislodged the flywheel from the main body. Then he came and told us frankly that he had no more interest in the engine. According to our agreement he had paid the company a deposit of one thousand five hundred shillings which was not refundable. He was prepared to forget about the deposit but we felt in fairness that half the amount should be refunded. He was very grateful.

There was yet another buyer. It was a father and son team, both very diminutive. They came late in the afternoon accompanied by two trucks, some ropes, a battered chain block and six labourers.

'*You* deal with all these engine buyers. I have too much paperwork to catch up with,' Rustam said to me.

I took them to the engine room and explained to them how other people had tried and failed. The old man, who must have been well over sixty, listened to me while the son walked around the engine, studying every component quietly. They would take it, they said.

That evening I told Rustam that I had struck a new type of bargain with the latest engine buyers. 'I have collected a thousand shillings from the old man. No deposit – no purchase price. They can take it or leave it.'

'You should not have done it. Did you see the tattered clothes the frail old man was wearing? They will have to struggle for a year to recover their thousand shillings.'

I too felt guilty. I said to Rustam that I would return the money the next morning.

Next morning old Mwasaru the storekeeper was waiting in our office with a look of a bereaved man.

'Bwana, someone has stolen that huge engine during the night.'

We rushed to the engine room. It was wiped clean. Not an ounce of metal was remaining in the room. Rustam and I burst out laughing. Mwasaru could not understand our behaviour. He was there when our father was operating the factory many years back. Give him a tiny pin to store and ten years later he would produce it. He had never in all his life lost a single item from the factory premises. Once he had misplaced a certain v-belt and we were very upset about it. And now a complete engine, weighing about ten tons, was missing and the bwanas were laughing with joy as if they had just won a sweepstake. Probably, life at Voi had driven them to *booza*.

We were still laughing when I saw Sheriff approaching us with a sly smile on his face. That meant trouble. I have never been able to understand why Sheriff found so much pleasure whenever there was any problem coming our way.

'Your Mr Adam is up to some mischief again.' Sheriff put extra emphasis on the word 'your'. This man always made us feel as if Adam were our naughty brother who kept on breaking all the neighbours' window panes and being a total nuisance to society.

To expect Adam not to be involved in some trouble was as unlikely as expecting a Hindu priest to admit that he had taken to cannibalism.

Apparently Adam had taken the dawn train to Mombasa

on a personal errand. Prior to boarding the dawn train he must have plastered himself thoroughly during the night. When the train arrived at Mombasa station he was still snoring in his compartment . . . lost to the world. After a reasonable interval, while the passengers are expected to disembark, the coaches are normally removed from the platform area and taken to the shunting yard for cleaning and servicing in preparation for the return journey to Nairobi in the evening. Adam was still asleep when the coaches were moved and a couple of sweepers carrying buckets and brooms entered his compartment. One of them was taken aback at the sight of a human form outstretched on a berth. 'I think we have a dead passenger.'

'More likely drunk than dead. Let us find out,' his companion replied. Then he emptied the bucket containing the dirty water on the sleeping man's face. Adam woke up with a start and could not register what was happening. Four curious eyes were staring at him. He looked through the compartment's window. The place was crowded with freight wagons and passenger coaches. Further up there was a small steam loco laboriously pushing half a dozen wagons. Only when Adam looked at his watch and realised what time it was did the reality begin to sink in. He now remembered boarding the early morning train at Voi.

'I overslept,' he remarked as he picked up his small bag and made his way past the two astonished sweepers. He jumped down into the shunting yard. Now all that remained was to figure out which way the platform lay. He jumped a few railway tracks in one direction, and then back again. It was becoming apparent that this way he would not get anywhere. He paused to think whether he should ask for assistance from a railway worker.

That was when a constable of the Railway Police picked him up.

His scruffy looks, dishevelled hair and water from the sweeper's bucket dripping down his chin did nothing to make him look respectable, while he explained his situation to the constable as convincingly as possible. But there was one major snag. He could not remember where he had put his ticket. The constable marched him to the Railway Police Station near the main station building. The OCS was not present so Adam was pushed into a cell. There was only one other occupant of the cell, a doped man lying flat on his back on the floor who took a fleeting look at Adam and went back to his dream world.

When the OCS came in a little later the constable brought Adam in front of him. He took a very, very long look at Adam and then smiled broadly.

'So you are the person who has been stealing all these potatoes?'

'Potatoes? What potatoes are you talking about?' This accusation was the unkindest cut for a man who had shot charging lion and elephant all his adult life. If he was accused of being involved in theft of gold bullion or diamonds there was at least some trace of respectability in it. But potatoes! Of all the commodities in this world, why potatoes?

'By the time we have finished with you, you will find out what potatoes we are talking about.' The OCS smiled triumphantly. Then he asked the constable to lock Adam up again until he came back from some other work.

During the OCS's absence Adam tried to talk some reason into the constable. He also asked him why his superior officer was so obsessed about potatoes. The constable began to see in Adam something more than a petty thief. He told Adam that an up-country vegetable grower had been complaining to the police that his consignments were always short in weight on arrival in Mombasa. The Railway Police were on the lookout for the culprit.

When the OCS returned Adam put a request to him:

'This is my driving licence. Why don't you put a telephone call to my employer at Voi and find out the truth?'

The constable nodded his head in sympathy and the result was Sheriff approaching us in the engine room, telling us there was a telephone call from Mombasa waiting in the office. The Railway Police wanted our management to confirm if a person with such and such a name and of such and such a description was in our employ.

All that was confirmed. Adam was set free.

After his humiliating experience at Mombasa Railway Station, Adam's fate seemed to be leading him into an even more unpleasant direction.

One day he was driving back to Voi from Nairobi. At noon he decided to have lunch from the picnic basket he was carrying. His family was with him and they drove off the main road into the bush and stopped under a huge shady tree. He was in a peaceful mood while eating and pointing out baboons to his son.

What Adam did not realise was that the shady tree was inside Tsavo National Park boundary . . . just by a few yards. To aggravate matters he had his guns in his vehicle with bullets in the magazines. Some junior game scouts on anti-poaching patrol happened to be passing by and noticed his vehicle. They were very upset when they realised that the owner of the vehicle also had loaded guns with him. Adam was asked to drive in front of them to the nearest game department . . . at Voi.

'Dougie' Walker's team at the Central Firearms Bureau in Nairobi were never appreciative of such irregularities. No amount of pleading helped Adam. All his guns were confiscated and sent to the central armoury at Gilgil for storage. His firearms certificate was withdrawn.

Adam was no longer a big game hunter.

'Never mind the guns. I can do other jobs.' Adam was a brave man and that quality in him was at least appreciable. He moved to Nairobi with his family but ill fortune was to follow him doggedly. This time in a literal sense.

There were not many jobs that fitted Adam's background. Ultimately, he landed himself a job as junior assistant to the duty officer of a major airline at what was known in those days as Nairobi International Airport (now Jomo Kenyatta International Airport). His job was to perform minor errands and do odd jobs for the duty officer.

Not long afterwards a wealthy South African businessman was flying to London. He decided to have his pet dog, a giant of a bull terrier named Zulu, to accompany him. He paid extra charges to see that Zulu was taken off the plane and taken for a short walk when the aircraft refuelled at Nairobi that night. The partially doped Zulu was taken out of the kennel and handed over to Adam to take for a walk within the perimeter of the airport. Now, either the dog was edgy from having been caged up for so long in a dark and humming atmosphere, or he might have smelled a bitch. Anyway, he darted, snatching the lead from Adam's grip and simply disappeared into the African darkness.

Adam was in one hell of a spot. For a few moments he did not know what to do. Then he had an idea. He rushed to the terminal building and rang a friend in the city.

'Get me a dog. Make it quick.'

'You have been drinking again, Adam,' his friend replied.

'Stop acting like an Anglican priest and listen to me.' Adam related the situation and his friend went looking for a dog.

He found one.

Unfortunately it was the tiniest and most sickly stray dog that could be found in the entire city of Nairobi. Adam's friend pounced on the poor thing as it was scavenging in a dustbin in the darkness somewhere in the slums of Eastleigh. Anyone standing within fifteen feet could count each rib of the starving dog. He put it in a basket and took a taxi ride to the airport.

'I said a dog! What is this?' Adam was justified in feeling frustrated.

'You didn't give me much time, did you!'

'Damn you!'

Adam had no choice. He quickly pushed the creature into the aircraft kennel. Somehow no one noticed the discrepancy as everyone was busy trying to get the plane ready for take-off. Soon the aircraft flew on to London.

When the South African was handed his dog in London he thought it was either a practical joke in poor taste or there was some bad mix-up. The papers were checked and rechecked. He was told it was his dog all right. First he became dumb. Then the giant man flared up into uncontrollable behaviour. He clobbered a couple of attendants at the animal terminal.

'This is not my Zulu. It is not even a dog. That damn thing there is a bloody rat!' He was thumping his powerful fists at everything in sight as the terrified airline staff, nursing their bloody noses, stood around helplessly. Then he sued the airline. The people in charge of animal airfreight launched an enquiry. The accusing finger stopped at Adam. The duty officer called Adam to his office.

'Tell me, Adam, I am most interested in how you can get things shrunk! My wife is complaining of her weight. Perhaps you can be of some help.'

Adam remained quiet.

'Speak up man!' The duty officer became impatient.

'Why pick on me if a dog goes through a biological change during that long flight between Johannesburg and London?'

'You stinking liar! Just because of you that ferocious *kaburu* is now shouting that everybody at Nairobi airport is a *Kaffir* of the worst kind.'

Adam lost his job. Then he decided to leave the country. The last I heard of him he was working as a storekeeper in an ammunition factory somewhere in North America. For the life of me I cannot but imagine that every time Adam sees a rifle bullet, he is reminded of his time at Tsavo when he was the master of a mighty and lethal piece of metal.

NINE

His name was Slau.

But everyone who knew him called him Chacha. His friends called him Chacha, his foes called him Chacha, his creditors called him Chacha (these were countless) – so we also called him Chacha.

When Chacha appeared on our scene, he gave us a different dimension to life. In his presence minor jokes became the cause for prolonged hilarity; an ordinary piece of music a major symphony. Evenings had more hue in the sky and at night we saw more stars than before. Morning ... well, after Chacha's coming all mornings were nothing but a series of bad hangovers. It was uncanny the way Chacha could 'borrow' fifty bob from you knowing that it would never be paid back. But no one minded that. The 'borrowed' sum would go towards the purchase of a bottle of whisky and Chacha made sure everyone shared it. Refusal would mean a mini riot. His philosophy was simple: rob Paul and don't pay Peter. Instead buy good whisky and some prime steak. As the night passed by and the bottle level dropped he would secretly add some water to 'keep the bottle alive'. In any event, who needed unadulterated whisky to be euphoric when he was around!

Six foot two inches tall, broad-shouldered and arms with the grip of a plumber's vice, in his younger days Chacha had represented his country in the Kenya Eleven, in what was then the most popular event in the soccer calendar of Eastern Africa: the Gossage Cup. He had also worked as a fireman on the coal-burning Garratt locomotives of the Kenya Uganda Railways. Once he had been downgraded in his railway job. It took me one year to get out of him the reason why. (He had been munching over fried chicken in the coal tender while the poor loco driver was struggling with an under-pressured locomotive on Kijabe Escarpment. Not once. Three times in a row!) In his younger days he had accompanied the legendary 'Simba Mbili' on hunting expeditions.

Simba Mbili's real name was Abdul Hamid Khan and he belonged to the generation of Indians who had migrated to Kenya in the early part of this century to work for the railway. The man too, was some sort of a giant, standing six and a half feet tall with wrists the size of an ordinary man's calf. He was a rail track inspector (or SPWI in railwayman's jargon). Once (if the legend is to be believed) the small complement of labourers pushing him on his inspection trolley unexpectedly ran into a large pride of lions somewhere around Tsavo River. He picked up his 10.75 rifle ('Puff Guns' as they were nicknamed because of their poor firing and trajectory power) and started dropping the surprised but upset lions – in American cowboy style.

That was the survival game one had to play in those days, when wild beasts roamed around as freely and in as many numbers as cattle and sheep. When he had brought down eleven lions with as many bullets he realised he had only one bullet left and there were still two angry beasts wanting to strike back at his entourage. The last bullet went through one of the beasts and sank into the brain of the second, killing both of them. Thus he earned the nickname of Simba Mbili (or 'Two Lions' translated from Kiswahili).

Regrettably his other experiences such as throttling a leopard which had strayed into his tent at night with his bare hands have remained undocumented. He was not always at the firing end. Once, while trying to retrieve a bird that he had shot, he came face to face with a Cape buffalo in thick bush. He was gored beyond recognition. For months on end he hovered between life and death and swore to have nothing more to do with any animals – not even a domestic cat. However, eventually, the call of the wild got the better of him and he went back to bush life together with his awkward gun. He died in 1955 at the ripe old age of ninety-five, drinking his bottle of gin a day right to the end.

A mutual friend was to tell me about Chacha's educational background. His father had also worked for the railways when Chacha was a young boy. His father used to get transferred from one station to another like other railway workers – but perhaps more often. Eventually, when the family came to Nairobi, Chacha was sent to a primary school. When the headmaster asked him to write on a piece of paper anything in English so they could judge which standard to place him in, Chacha wrote: A B C D E F G H.

'What is this you have written?' he was asked.

'English!' Chacha replied.

'English! We do not think that embraces the entire language. Do you know anything besides this?'

Chacha replied. 'No sir!'

'You look like a big boy. How long have you been studying?'

'Three years, sir!'

'You mean to say in three years this is all you learnt?'

'How can I help it? Every time I learnt the alphabet up to the letter 'H' my father got transferred. At every new school I was grouped with pupils beginning to learn A B C D.'

Chacha walked with a slight, almost unnoticeable limp. He was the fireman on duty on a freight train hauling mixed cargo from the western highlands to Nairobi one night.

About ten minutes before reaching Equator Station some 8,600 feet above sea level, the loco driver noticed a drop in the air pressure system operating the train's brakes. (Unlike in most countries, where brakes operate on a vacuum system, ours operate on a pressure system because of the high altitudes the rail lines pass through.)

The normal drill was for the fireman to come out of the cab and walk out in the open on the narrow platform along the boiler holding a hammer to bash the steam-operated compressor pump, while the train pushed on. With this sort of stuntmanship, usually a clogged valve would start refunctioning. Chacha did this, that chilly night, and when he returned to the cab he developed an uncontrollable shiver. At Equator Station he was put into the 'running room' while the station master went looking for a doctor. There was no doctor available but the local veterinary surgeon volunteered to help. Fortunately he had a phial of anti-pyretic, but the only syringes he had were the ones he used for cattle. He pushed one into Chacha's bottom. Chacha was cured – but left with a small limp and a lifelong ugly habit of being abusive to any vet he ever met.

Later in life he had taken up hunting professionally. He started conducting his own safaris and, by the time he came to Voi, he was well established with overseas clientele. Wildlife hunting safaris in Kenya were in vogue in those days. He wanted to establish a permanent camp on the company's land. He had selected a site at the foot of Signal Hill with a commanding view of the plains of Tsavo in the west. The hill had earned itself this name because some time in the past there was a steel tower erected by the police, from where they relayed their radio messages.

'You can establish the camp provided you do animal control work for the company whenever required, and without charge.' That was our condition.

'Look now, that is OK with me,' spoke Chacha. No, he never spoke. The man used to thunder. And I have yet to remember Chacha starting a sentence without using the words 'Look now'.

He was given a company house into which he and his family settled. Thus Chacha came to Voi – and to give us a different dimension to life. If I imagine him to have been larger than life then that is because he *was* larger than life.

As soon as he had settled his family in the company's house, he started building his camp. He sent his trucks to the riverside to collect rough stones to be used as basic construction material. Gradually small huts, kitchen, bathroom, mess, etc, began to take some sort of shape. If the mess-room was wider by three feet at one end when compared to the other it did not matter. 'Does it bother you?' he would ask if we pointed out the error.

Asymmetrical or shapeless mess-room, the camp began to be the centre of our social lives. Whenever he had hunting clients he would have their dinner served early in the evening and get them pushed to their beds.

'Look now, we have to start early in the morning. Better take enough rest.' His clients would be asleep by half past eight.

Then he would join us by the log fire near his kitchen. Chacha would now take out a joint of prime beef from the fridge. A whisky bottle would be unwrapped from an old newspaper. He would hold the bottle in front of his eyes and look at it intently for a few seconds before unscrewing it.

I wish I could have found out what flashed through his mind during those few seconds he looked at the bottle. The evening would now begin and the camp fire would burn late into the night.

Chacha's clients ranged from the finest hunters to the phoniest hunters. While some of them might have shot polar bears in the Arctic region or a tiger in India there would be those who would beg Chacha to bring the animal down for them. Lots of photographs would be taken to show friends back home what it was like to be in Africa hunting big game. One client could not distinguish the sex of the animal. He kept on shooting down female eland which is illegal. After Chacha had literally buried his clients third blunder he was politely told to leave his hunting to Chacha himself.

Then there was a wealthy Frenchman who was Chacha's regular client. He was always accompanied by his comely wife and a teenage daughter. Invariably he came in the month of October and selected the time to establish himself in the camp a day or two before full moon. He never made an attempt to shoot at any animal. Occasionally he would make a token round of the hunting area and at best, he would shoot a tiny dik dik before insisting on returning to the camp. On the actual night of the full moon he would take his elephant gun out of its canvas cover and load it with ammunition. As soon as the moon appeared, rising over Signal Hill, he would take careful aim and shoot at it. He would fire at the rising moon at random intervals until about ten o'clock. Then he would go to sleep. Having repeated the performance for the next two or three days he would shift to a beach hotel in Mombasa for a time before flying back to his business in France. Whenever he was asked about his behaviour there was only one answer.

'It gives me enormous pleasure.'

'Why does it give you pleasure?'

'I have my private reasons.'

I never discovered why this man wanted to shoot the moon down.

Nobody who spent time at Chacha's camp at the foot of Signal Hill could forget the breathtaking and panoramic view at that spot. Below the camp the land tapered down to plains that extended as far as the eye could see. In the evenings, as the sun sank and the sky shifted to different hues, it became, at times, difficult to distinguish between land and sky. They simply merged into each other. In pre-Christopher Columbus times mankind believed that at the far edge of the ocean was the end of the world. If a sailor sailed that far he would drop down into a bottomless dark hollow, into a type of abyss. Occasionally, when I took time to watch the plains stretching to embrace the sky on the horizon I felt like saying: that really is the end of the world.

Many old-timers have been known to refer to such heavenly views as MMBA. That is their abbreviation for 'Miles and Miles of Bloody Africa'. What I cannot accept is why be so derogative about such a priceless sight? Why not 'Miles and Miles of Beloved Africa'? Or even 'Miles and Miles of Beautiful Africa'?

This remote corner of the world became our personal centre of the universe. This was our theatre and Chacha was the central character. This camp was the scene of many happenings.

The camp was a scene of surprise.

Chacha normally travelled to Nairobi whenever his clients were coming, in order to collect them direct from the airport.

Before driving back to Voi he would pick up vegetables, rations, tinstuff and a handful of friends. So, in the evenings, Chacha's camp was not inhabited only by three or four foreign clients who spoke little English and knew even less about Africa, but, at the far end of the mess was another group of people – his companions from Nairobi, some of our friends from Voi, and some of Chacha's own workmates.

Kariga was a good cook and we were good eaters. Having seen his clients to bed, Chacha would join us, usually grumbling about the behaviour of his clients:

'That fool Andre van Marne took a pot-shot at a cobra with his rifle. Luckily he did not miss. We would have been in a mess.'

One day he came back a little late from Nairobi. He was accompanied by two distinguished looking Italian gentlemen and a pretty lady. The lady's face was familiar but no one could place her.

'Look now, who we have here.' Chacha started introducing the lady to the few residents who were at the camp. The group could not believe its eyes. The lady was Gina Lollobrigida!

Later on in the night when the party was well settled in the camp Chacha was drawn aside and asked:

'What is she doing here in Voi?'

'I met her at a party in Nairobi and told her I could bag a bongo for her.'

'You said what?'

'I could shoot a bongo for her,' Chacha replied without the slightest hint of guilt.

'A bongo? Here around Voi?'

'Look now, you know there are no bongoes here and I know there are no bongoes here. Does she also have to know?'

The lady got no bongo. That did not seem to perturb her. At night when dinner had been served and everyone sat around the camp fire she would join the local women in traditional dancing. She did it with utmost ecstacy. The camp fire burnt late into the night.

The camp was the scene of occasional embarrassments.

Mr Bernardi, a client of Chacha, had shot a lion. It was a large Masai lion with a jet black mane. The shooting was no easy job either. The animal was injured when they first shot at him and the wounded creature had disappeared into the bush. Chacha and his client tracked him for nearly half an hour under tense conditions, until they finally got him.

That night there was a big celebration in the mess. Bernardi's wife was also present. She was a rotund woman of robust figure – the finished product of a lifelong love affair with spaghetti. Lots of champagne was flowing and everyone was hugging and kissing each other. Mr Bernardi was more high than the others. Then he did what should have been discreetly reserved for some other occasion, for he said loudly:

'Salina, I need you. You must come and see what I have shot. O Salina where are you . . .?'

His wife's first name was not Salina. Everyone stopped talking and shouting. The spaghetti woman shot up from her chair – all purple, from top to bottom. She started barking at her husband in their vernacular. Whatever she was saying could not have been pleasant. Mr Bernardi quickly sobered up and sat down in his chair, all colour drained from his face.

The spaghetti woman would not let it go at that. She walked up to her husband across the table and started bashing him with her handbag while still shouting. The husband defended his head with his hands and went on accepting the punishment without any protest. Others intervened and separated them. We all sat in the mess for about ten embarrassing minutes until the woman ordered her husband to their tent. He followed her timidly.

Next morning the watchman told Chacha that Mr Bernardi's tent was all shouts and screams the whole night. Mr Bernardi must have thought: better face a lion than this old windbag.

The camp was the scene of ingenious ideas.

One evening we brought up the subject of wheel springs for the sisal trailers. Too many springs used to break into pieces because of potholes in the roads leading to the sisal blocks.

Chacha said:

'Why do you have to have springs in a sisal trailer? Sisal leaves are not human beings. They cannot feel the jolts.'

'Then why are they placed there in the first place?' I asked him.

'So that the manufacturers of these trailers can make extra profit by selling spares.'

We remained silent for a moment. I wondered if Chacha's reasoning had any validity.

Next day we decided to be a little unorthodox about mechanics and asked Lofty to try fixing the wheel axle direct to the chassis of a trailer. This was to be our experimental model.

The last trailer of the day bringing sisal from the field used to be only half loaded so that the sisal cutters could hitch a ride back to the labour camp near the factory.

About eight or ten cutters were sitting on top of the sisal bundles in the experimental springless trailer, coming back home in the evening. They were in their normal jovial mood after the day's work. A couple of them were singing in their native tongue. One was wrapping tobacco in a small cutting of newspaper, preparing for his long awaited puff. One or two were simply lying on the bundles. One was drinking the last drop of maize meal porridge from his flask. Thus they were all preoccupied so they never found out what it was that tossed them suddenly skywards and back onto the ground. The pothole must have been a nasty one.

Fortunately nobody was badly hurt. They were mighty angry though. A few of them suggested that they should chop off Lofty's right ankle so that he could never fiddle around with the trailer again. One of them had lost a shoe, for which he went looking the next three days, without any success.

Chacha avoided us for a long time.

The camp was the scene of high infidelity.

Chacha had four to five safaris scheduled in a row during the coming two months. He had to be in Nairobi for about four days to prepare for these safaris. Tents required repairing, ammunition had to be bought, necessary papers and permits had to be obtained from the Game Department.

Meanwhile he had one couple at the camp who had come for a ten-day photographic safari. He decided to sub-contract this safari to a pair of freelancing hunters, Yacob and his partner, 'Brother' Harry, and left his clients, Mr and Mrs Lowe, in their charge.

'Take good care of them. They look prospective clients for the future,' Chacha requested before leaving.

That was a tragic arrangement. Mr Lowe was sixty-five years old, if he was a day. His wife, Monica, could not have celebrated her twenty-fifth birthday. She was a blonde with sparkling blue eyes. Her body movements were enticing – like a tigress on perpetual heat.

To look after them were Yacob and Harry. Yacob was a responsible and respected married man. Not so 'Brother' Harry. He was an irresponsible, reckless and handsome phil-andering bachelor. His real name was not Harry either. Every time he went back to his parents in Nairobi after a safari he became 'mama's good boy' and was called by his actual name.

Even before Chacha had reached Nairobi, Harry had started making advances to Monica. She responded with secret smiles. That night between the two of them they did a cruel thing. They put sleeping tablets in Mr Lowe's coffee. Even before the dessert was over Mr Lowe's forehead had dropped onto the table. He was helped to bed by his wife and Harry, while Yacob walked to the other tent, meant for him and Harry. A little later Harry came to this tent in the company of his lady.

'What is she doing here?' Yacob had some premonition. He had known Harry long enough.

'She is going to teach me French.'

'No, she is not. Not in our tent while I am asleep.' Yacob was blunt.

'I don't think you ought to sleep here. You will be dis-turbed unnecessarily. You know how unpleasant these French pronunciations are.'

'Oh yes, I know about your French lessons! This is not the first time you have tried to learn a foreign language. What do you suggest I do?'

'Here, take some extra blankets and a bottle of cognac. Go and share the tent with the cook.'

'You must be joking,' Yacob said.

'Please try to be understanding,' Harry pleaded.

After a lengthy argument, while the young woman sat in a chair filing her nails, unconcerned, Yacob decided to let Harry do whatever he wanted. He went to spend the night in the cook's tent. He could hear giggling and laughter in their tent. Learning French indeed, he thought, before falling asleep.

At about two in the morning Mr Lowe came running out of his tent. He was enquiring at the top of his voice.

'Has anyone seen my wife?'

The stillness of the night was shattered. The workers woke up and came out of their tents. Yacob and the cook joined the group that was now surrounding Mr Lowe, who was still in an agitated state. This commotion was long enough for Harry to help the young lady slip back into her tent. He then joined the group and tactfully led Mr Lowe back to it.

'What is the matter, darling?' Mrs Lowe enquired, yawning widely.

'I think I am having bad dreams.'

Next morning Mr Lowe was taken to photograph his animals and could scarcely hold his camera steady.

At noon they were standing on a huge rock. Mr Lowe was trying to focus on Cape buffalo some half a mile away with his telephoto lens. Then the sleepy man did a stupid thing. He dropped the camera. It went crashing down the rock to the ground thirty feet below, and one of his expensive Japanese cameras was reduced to a useless assortment of dented metal and cracked glass.

That evening back at the camp, Yacob warned Harry.

'Don't do this inhuman thing to the man. You will kill him. If that happens, Chacha will wring our necks.'

'You worry too much. It is not good for your health,' Harry replied.

'My health? What about the health of that poor unsuspecting foreigner!'

That night the sleeping pills were slipped in Mr Lowe's beer to be on the safe side. Towards morning Yacob woke up from his sleep. There was someone speaking outside the cook's tent.

Mr Lowe was sitting on a small boulder a little further away. He was looking up at the sky and murmuring, 'Kenya coffee no good; Kenya beer no good; Kenya climate no good . . .' Yacob went back to sleep, feeling rotten.

On the third night, despite Yacob's strong protest the malicious act was repeated. Yacob did not attend dinner. He had developed a bad cold and cough despite the extra blankets and cognac, and went to sleep early. Mr Lowe did not wake up during the night to enquire if his wife was still around, nor to complain to God about all those rotten things of Kenya. In fact, he did not wake up even in the morning. When his head was lifted he would open his eyes and beg to be left alone to go back to sleep. There was something more sinister. He had developed an unusual symptom. Yacob insisted on having him taken to the local hospital immediately.

The doctor at the hospital was confused.

'Has this happened to your husband before?'

'Not to my knowledge,' his wife replied.

'Does he drink to the point of losing consciousness each night?' The doctor wanted to learn all about his patient's behaviour.

'No, he drinks very moderately,' Mrs Lowe replied.

'Does he mix sleeping pills with his drinks?'

'We don't carry any sleeping pills.'

The doctor rested his chin on his right palm as he looked at his helpless patient. Then he said:

'I cannot understand the cause of this incontinence. It is time to see a specialist when a person suddenly begins to lose control over his bladder during sleep. Lady, I suggest you take your husband back to where you came from.'

The safari came to a premature and abrupt end.

Chacha arrived back from Nairobi the next evening. For a few seconds he was speechless at the sight of the deserted camp. Then he thundered:

'Why is the camp dead, where are all the workers? Where are my clients? Look now, will somebody tell me what has been happening here?'

The two figures sitting on upturned empty beer crates did not reply. One of them was too preoccupied coughing, sneezing and blowing his nose with a handkerchief. The other simply stared at Chacha not knowing exactly how to explain to him what had happened to his clients.

But Chacha was not all whisky, fun and carefreeness. He, too, had a personal life and pains. Once he took a couple of German clients for two days' safari some seventy miles away. He returned to Voi only hours before his two-year-old son died. The child had suddenly been taken ill while Chacha was out hunting. He had loved Micky very much.

There was no camp fire at the foot of Signal Hill for a long time then.

TEN

Chacha was laughing heartily. It was a Sunday morning. His next safari was six weeks away. Whenever there were long breaks between safaris, Chacha moved in and joined his family in the house provided by the company. In the compound was a tamarind tree. Under this tree Chacha would arrange his safari chair, stretch his legs and while away his time. In the evenings he always prepared a charcoal fire on a home-made oven. The inevitable choice cut of beef would be brought out, his special spices would be sprinkled over it, and on top of this he added enough chilli powder for the manufacture of a small sized canister of tear gas. The grilled meat that finally came out from the oven was called *tikki*. Chacha relished his *tikkis* but others barely survived the night. Once a Belgian client unsuspectingly took a bite of a *tikki* and the local doctor had to keep the poor man's mouth plastered with glycerine for two days.

'My father ate *tikki* all his life. And do you know how long he lived?' Chacha asked us once.

'No, how long?'

'Until he died,' Chacha replied. His father must have either been big and strong like Chacha himself, or he could not have lived to celebrate his fortieth birthday. No, not with this stuff – one's guts would become perforated.

Other people's shortcomings were often a source of

amusement for Chacha and this time his laughter was for Mr Hugo, the company's new mechanic.

Lofty had retired and we had Hugo as our new diesel mechanic. Between Lofty's departure and Hugo's settling in there were quite a few mechanics who had come and gone. Some of them did not like us, and there were others whom we could not accept. One of them – I think his name was Imam Bux – was not only a bad mechanic, but I was convinced he was also a downright mental case. If a machine refused to work after having been repaired he would shout and swear at it – just the way a foreman swears at a worker who has committed an unforgivable blunder.

'Instead of getting angry, why do you not find out what is wrong in there?' we suggested to him.

'You don't know them well enough. They are the most ungrateful of all creations of mankind,' he replied, spitting on the ground.

One day he made a very bad job of setting a tractor's timing gears and the tractor simply refused to start. When Imam Bux realised his shouting and spitting was not producing any results, he got another tractor to pull the defaulting tractor while he sat on the latter's controls trying to jump-start it. Not only did he go on swearing, but he was whipping the machine with a branch of a tree. Rustam stood there shaking his head in astonishment. They had towed the sick tractor some two miles deep into the sisal fields when its exhaust coughed out a ball of flame almost in protest. The resultant fire burnt down seventy acres of sisal.

'Go, Imam Bux – or whatever your name is – go. Life is sticky enough as it is.'

Later I was to learn that he liked to get a little high on opium.

Thus Hugo became our new mechanic. He had previously worked on diesel engines in the wheat growing area of West Kilimanjaro. He was a quiet, unassuming bachelor. By any standard he was a good mechanic as far as diesel engines were concerned. He had one problem though.

Some fifteen days after he had started working, a tractor driver reported to him that his oil pressure gauge was registering 'zero'. Hugo checked the electric cable leading to the gauge for a faulty connection. No, that was not the cause. A blocked oil filter or an oil pipe could be the culprit – it was neither of those. Hugo decided to open the sump of the engine. Inside the sump lay broken pieces of shaft that drove the oil pump.

That was when Hugo started sneezing.

First the sneezes came at intervals of a few seconds. Then they became more frequent. By the time we were informed that our mechanic was somewhat unwell Hugo was having uncontrollable fits of sneezing. He gestured to us to take him home. Inside a drawer at his home he pulled out a small bottle of tablets and gulped some down. After about five minutes the sneezing had subsided to a certain extent. Within half an hour he was back on the job to see that a new shaft from the store had replaced the broken one. He still had the odd sneeze as he worked, but the situation was not bad enough to make him unable to repair the tractor.

The day we had a major breakdown in a tractor, Hugo's sneezing bouts did not start with moderate intervals. The moment he realised that a broken valve had lodged itself between the piston and the cylinder head, causing the latter to crack, he went into a blind rage of sneezing. He literally had to be carried to his house and to his tablets.

'If it is an allergy, we don't know about it,' the doctor said. 'It may be a psychomotor case. Take him to a good psychiatrist.'

Call it occupational hazard of a plantation manager – Hugo was a fine young mechanic who could not face broken down machines. And Chacha loved to poke fun at such characters.

"You find it the object of fun when someone behaves strangely or acts stupidly, Chacha, but what if you make idiotic mistakes yourself! Don't you think you too belong to the same class?" Rustam asked Chacha. " What about that warm night as a fireman of the train to Mombasa?"

All of us, including Chacha, laughed aloud. We were referring to the time when he had just joined the railway service after a handful of riff-raff jobs having left a somewhat sketchy schooling. He was lucky to apply for the job with the Railways when he did. His first job was in the loco shed. The person whose job Chacha got had to leave the Railway services under some very bizarre circumstances. This man was a person of few words. He was always punctual in reporting for work and was one of the finest craftsmen in the loco shed. One day he unexpectedly went berserk. He picked up a ten-pound hammer and started swinging it menacingly.

"What is your problem, Hassan, why are you behaving like that?" Other workers asked him from a safe distance.

He said he wanted to break open the skulls of all white workers of the Railway. "I want the white people to compensate for taking away *Kohi Noor* diamond from India".

"Look mister, we have nothing to do with political issues of India. We are here to see the smooth running of the railway." The white loco shed foreman shouted at him from the far corner of the shed. When the insanely behaving person was slightly off guard, the other workers pounced upon him and subdued him.

It later emerged that for some mysterious reason he had been very high on opium on that particular day.

He was handed over to the police. In the court he told the magistrate that he would never again have anything to do with opium and would not swing a hammer menacingly. But he was adamant that the whites should compensate Indians for taking away the *Kohi Noor*. He was given a year and a half.

Chacha had applied for the job at the time when our hammer-swinging hero had lost his job. He began as a junior spanner boy. But in a few years he rose through ranks and file to become a loco fireman.

One particular evening he was the first-shift fireman on a passenger train from Nairobi to Mombasa. He finished his duty at midnight and returned to his compartment in caboose coach. Such coaches were meant for the relief crews of the train when they were off duty. The coaches had no corridor between cabins, with the door of each compartment opening straight to the outside. These caboose coaches were attached to the rear end of the train.

He was hungry and opened the Tiffin that contained mutton curry and rice that his mother had prepared for him. He realized that it was too hot in there. To make the matter worse the cabin fan was not working. He opened every window of the cabin and removed his pajama top without much joy. Then he had an ingenious idea. He opened the cabin door and sat on the threshold of the cabin, legs dangling out in the open. Then he began to dig his fingers into the Tiffin. Ah, that is good, he thought. What he had ignored were the laws of physics. The train took a slight turn to the left. The heavy cabin door came swinging on to his back.

He was catapulted out into the African bush, still holding on to his Tiffin.

It took sometime for the realisation to sink into him. Soon he saw the red light at the back of the Guard's van disappear into the dark. The train was gone.....minus him. This is terrible, he thought. He was stranded in the middle of a wild game area in the middle of the night. Soon he began to hear the cries and roars of animals from surrounding areas. Well, this is it, he said to himself. He knew that no one would miss him until the train had reached Mombasa the next morning. It won't be long before these carnivorous animals get me. Oh God, if you are there, please do come and help me, Chacha prayed.

Tim Black was pushing his train up a gradient at full power. He was already two hours late and wanted to make up for the lost time. His Garrett *EC 3* steam loco was doing its best. Suddenly he thought he saw something very unusual in the powerful beam of the locomotive's arc lamp.

"Do you see what I see, Dilbag?" He asked his fireman loudly over the noise of the machine. Dilbag stretched his eyes and replied. "I think there is a man standing by the line."

Tim Black cut down on power and slowed down and when they had reached the man standing by the line, he stopped the train.

"What on blooming earth is that Indian *Fakir* doing in middle of the African wild with his begging bowl! Well I will be damned! Look after the machine as I go and see what that unearthly person is up to, Dilbag"

He came face to face with Chacha and said. "Do you realise that this is a very fierce place to be, and all alone, whatever your name is mister!"

"I believe so." Chacha replied.

"What is that in that pot you are holding in your hand?" Tim Black inquired.

"Mutton curry and rice that my mother had prepared and I was about to eat. That's when…"

"What is the idea of wearing pajama minus its top? Do you belong to some secret voodoo cult that move around with their magic charms?"

"I like to eat my dinner in my pajama so I can go to sleep soon afterwards. Actually it was the blooming cabin door…." Chacha was confused as to how to explain the situation. "Oh never mind. Let me start from the beginning. I was about to start eating. The door was behind me. I did not realize………."

The engine driver's patience had come to an end and he did not want to waste any more time. "Your mother……Cabin door……rice and mutton curry…..moving around at night minus the pajama top while holding a pot. No, honestly all this does not add up. Are you sure everything is o.k. up there with you?" Then turning to his fireman he said above the noise of the rumbling firebox inferno: "Did you know Dilbag, that there is one born every minute?"

Getting back to Nairobi was the finest thing that ever happened to Chacha.

We were still laughing heartily at this episode in Chacha's life when his tone changed. We knew he had something on his mind, which he wanted to tell us.

'I don' know if I should take this'. Chacha handed Rustam a letter. Chacha's latest clients had left earlier in the day. Rustam and I were sitting with Chacha as he supervised the 'closing down' of the camp. Chacha's staff worked while he stretched his legs after two weeks of cross-country driving and walking with the clients. Chacha sipped his whisky and told Rustam about a suggestion from a friend in Nairobi. The letter indicated, amongst other things, that a very prominent film producer in India was in Nairobi and was looking for a professional hunter to assist in one or two hunting scenes. Would Chacha be interested, the friend in Nairobi was enquiring.

'Why, what is wrong with it? Is the money not enough?' Rustam asked Chacha.

'Money would hardly be the problem. I don't know about these Bombay movie-makers. Instinctively I have misgivings about them.'

'Take this up, Chacha. If you can face a charging lion you might as well face the Indian movie-makers.'

'I think I shall,' said Chacha. 'In any event, I have no safaris for the next two months.'

And so the movie-maker crowd arrived at Chacha's camp. They had come with all the necessary papers from the Game Department. A strict vegetarian diet had to be adhered to and a couple of translators had to be found as none of the visitors knew a word of Kiswahili except *jambo*, *habari* and *mzuri*, which they pronounced *majuri*. No matter how much Chacha's staff tried to correct them they could not twist their tongues to pronounce the word correctly. The team consisted of the producer, director, various camera and sound technicians, a few extras, and, of course, the hero of the movie himself and his girlfriend – the daughter of a wealthy Indian industrialist.

One particular scene in which Chacha's assistance was required was when, in the movie plot, the hero comes across a rogue elephant. He casually shoots him down and sits on the beast and belches out a song. No Indian movie is worth a counterfeit rupee if it does not have a song at the most dramatic moment!

Actually Chacha had to do the physical shooting from a spot out of focus of the camera while the hero was pictured aiming the gun and firing at the animal. (This practice of actually shooting at wildlife while filming has long since been prohibited by the government.) It was some sort of trick photography.

None of the film team had seen Africa before let alone a wild African elephant. So it was arranged that they be taken on a familiarisation tour of the National Park, during which everyone saw a wild elephant for the very first time. Late that night Chacha was sitting near the kitchen, devouring his meal. The hero came and sat next to him. For a few moments he remained quiet. Then he asked:

'What do elephants do?'

Chacha looked at the actor for a moment not knowing what sort of question that was.

'What do elephants do?' he repeated.

'They eat leaves from trees, and walk, and have a mud bath, and reproduce, and die when they are old. What else did you expect them to do – form some sort of political party?'

The actor hesitated. 'Do they bite people?'

'No, they don't bite people. Crush them to death, yes, but they don't bite.'

The hero walked back to his tent gnawing at his nails. This man is going to be difficult, thought Chacha, as he went on munching his food.

So the shooting for this particular scene started. Chacha led the team to a few hunting blocks for a couple of days. Unfortunately, they did not find the lone bull the director was looking for. Either the elephants were in groups, or there would be a companion she-elephant with a calf. Eventually the team found a bull in nearby Masinga. It was an ideal situation. Hurriedly and quietly the cameras and other instruments were positioned in a spot Chacha selected where the wind was in their favour. All that was now remaining was for the actor to walk with Chacha within shooting range.

This is where the problem began to develop.

The actor would not step down from the vehicle. The

director approached him and whispered something in his ear while the actor kept on shaking his head. The producer joined them. The actor shook his head even more vigorously. A few others joined the murmuring group. Eventually the actor stepped down, accepted the gun that was handed to him, and joined Chacha. There were three more people with the actor. Chacha had become quite impatient by now. He spoke as softly as he could.

'Why is there a mob of people here? We want to shoot an elephant, not lynch him.'

'The director has agreed to the actor's request. He will feel more comfortable if a few of us friends are right behind him,' said one of them.

Chacha made no comment. He had come to the end of his tether.

The group walked softly towards the elephant. The actor had the look of a man being led to the gallows. Chacha motioned the group to a halt at the appropriate spot. He spoke in undertones to the actor: 'All you have to do now is to level your gun at that elephant. We are all standing a few paces behind you. The moment you aim your gun I will shoot him down. In the name of Lord Krishna, please just relax a little more.'

For the life of him, our hero could not hold his gun in a stable position. It swung in all directions, sometimes in circles, sometimes from side to side, or up and down. The cameras with their telephoto lenses kept on clicking from a distance.

'For God's sake steady yourself, mister. You will get us all killed if you insist on dangling that gun all day.' Chacha was positively angry. The elephant had now suspected something. It ceased munching grass and started flapping its ears.

By one chance in a hundred, the hero had his gun pointed for an instant. That very moment Chacha let his .458 Magnum go. The bullet found the vital spot. The animal just slumped to the ground. Chacha fired a couple more rounds for good measure.

Now the cameras stopped clicking. The directors and others approached the scene. Our hero was sitting on the ground, his two companions wiping his forehead and arms.

'O Ram, O Ram, O Ram!' Suddenly Chacha cried aloud. He was quite pliable with his language. He had just noticed something unusual that had been overlooked during all that fuss.

'What is this "O Ram" business in times of trouble?' The director was on the verge of tears.

'I don't know how you are going to explain it to your viewers, but your hero has just shot an elephant with a twelve bore shotgun. You cannot shoot even a small buck with that.'

After the flurry had died down it was now time for the hero to sit on the elephant and sing the song.

'No, I am not doing that. I don't care if the elephant *is* dead.' He came out with his feelings openly.

'Remember your terms of contract,' the producer shouted at him.

'The topmost lawyers in Bombay are my best friends,' shot back the actor even louder.

There were more consultations and arguments. Chacha got his trackers to cut the tail off the elephant and hand it over to the actor to prove that the elephant was now beyond any capacity to crush or bite him. After lengthy arguments and a lot of persuasion the actor agreed to sit on the back of the dead animal and sing his love song. His face could not have been more expressionless. Both the director and the producer shook their heads in despair.

The next day it was the same story all over again. The national park authorities maintained an animal orphanage near their administrative quarters, and there was a baby rhino in this orphanage, as tame as a domestic cat. The hero was to ride on this small creature and blow yet another song while the cameras rolled.

Nothing doing!

The argument lasted for hours. To ease the actor's fears Chacha sat on the back of this friendly rhino, followed by his tracker, and a few other staff of the orphanage. In the end, even the director of the movie team rode on the rhino hoping the hero could be persuaded to follow suit. Some time towards evening the actor agreed to a ninety second ride.

I am not sure if the movie was ever completed. If it was, it was never screened in Kenya . . .

ELEVEN

Then we were hit by the drought.

Normally the temperature begins to rise from January onwards until about mid-March when the intertropical convergence zone passes over Kenya on its way to the northern hemisphere. During an ordinary year it is then that the 'long rains' start.

That year January was comparatively cold. So was February and so was March.

'It looks like a bad year,' I mentioned to Rustam in mid-March.

'It *is* bad,' he said apprehensively.

In the second week of April we got some rain. The total for the month was one inch and three quarters. That was the end of our rainy season. May, June, and July were all dry months. They normally are, every year. The landscape began to change. In average years the vegetation would turn from lush green following the previous rains, to pale green, to yellowish green, then to brown. At that stage fresh rains would normally come to our rescue to complete the cycle. This year when the landscape became brown it remained that way. It had no colour left into which to change because there was no more vegetation. The red soil of Tsavo and shrivelled sisal plants took the last stand.

There was something else unusual about this year too. There

were too many elephants. For about a year and a half we had been hearing whispers: 'Too many elephants in Tsavo', or 'they will outnumber themselves,' or 'there are four elephants in an area where there is usually one'.

Since monitoring elephant population was not our business we had paid little attention to these whispers. Now we had been pushed into a situation where we had every reason to give credence to such veiled talk. This was no empty social gossip. We had lived long enough on the doorsteps of the park to believe that there were, in fact, too many elephants.

One American naturalist once said: 'Don't worry about too many elephants. One single bad drought will take care of that.'

This, then, was that 'one single bad drought'. By July groups of elephants started paying regular visits to small-scale farmers around Voi. They crushed their banana plants and had a field day with whatever little maize the farmers had managed to salvage during this dry year. The poor farmers had taken months of beating under the angry sun to raise these crops. One day the food was there. The next day it was not. As plain as that. Three months' hard work would dissolve during a night. The farmers and their families sat on the ground in despondency. Poverty . . . hunger . . . lack of school fees . . . These were the brief items people skipped through before turning to the sports pages of their newspapers. At that particular place and at that particular time those were the realities. In whatever direction one turned away, one could not avoid looking straight towards those facts.

Perhaps the Game Department could help out . . .

The game warden was sitting on a chair in his office, his forehead resting on the top of his desk. He slowly lifted his head. 'You are asking me how I can help the situation?' It was evident from his eyes that he had not slept for days. 'My men and myself have just driven back from Taveta.'

Taveta is a village seventy miles west of Voi, a potential banana-growing area because of various water flows.

'You should see how the situation is there. The elephants have completely flattened whole banana fields. For three days and nights my scouts have tried to keep these animals at bay. We tried to scare them away by firing in the air, shooting them, chasing them – you name it. They are too hungry to be deterred. They keep on coming like locusts. This is not the type of situation where the Game Department alone can do the job. Yes, perhaps a small battalion from the army and their rapid firing guns could help. Now, tell me, how do you want me to help?'

Next came the thirst:

The railway authorities had constructed a large water catchment on one of the hills surrounding Voi. The water flowed down through a pipe to Voi railway station. The steam locomotives were always thirsty. Every train that went between Mombasa and Nairobi consumed thousands of gallons of water at Voi Station. The pipe from the catchment passed through minor settlements, and people there drew their small share of water for domestic purposes.

For the first time in the memory of these residents the catchment had no water to offer. It had become bone dry. The steam locomotive slogged on for another twenty-nine miles to quench its thirst at Tsavo Station beside the Tsavo River. People in our area had no such alternative. Women and children began to make an eighteen-mile round trip, journeying on foot to fetch a four gallon container of water from Voi township. Walking that distance in a high temperature was no pleasant task.

Nature was benevolent in one particular instance. There was one well in the entire division that contained as much water as people could consume. Clean, fresh, precious water. People of the Voi Division rose to the occasion. Someone brought in a portable diesel operated pump. Others brought in empty drums and trucks. Yet one other person came along with a mobile tanker. Water was pumped out. The drums and the tanker were filled and taken to settlements. People at these settlements waited quietly and in orderly queues to receive their share of water. Not once did anyone take more water than was allocated. Not a single soul jumped the queue. In a month and a half over a million gallons of water were ferried to the thirsty population. On Sundays the water convoys started a little later, thus allowing the people in the settlements to attend church services. They prayed to God for rain and thanked Him for the well that refused to run dry while the country was scorched under the merciless sun. Some elders even prayed: 'Let the passing of time not make us forget the tireless and selfless efforts of those who keep the water flowing. Let memories not be shortlived.'

That was also the year the company lost the Masinga section of the plantation.

Serious problems were not unanticipated. But what followed was beyond our wildest imaginations. Chacha was stationed at Masinga area to control the hungry beasts. One day we were sitting in the office with a couple of travelling salesmen who were trying to sell us welding rods at a special price. Chacha barged into the office in a very agitated state, swinging his rifle in his hand.

'I will not do any more killing – for love or money.' Chacha was almost barking.

The salesmen did not know about our elephant problems, so I could hardly blame them for not understanding what the angry man holding a gun meant. They left in a hurry without so much as leaving their business cards.

'Sit down Chacha, we knew it was not going to be easy.'

'If you want me to do the control work, both of you will have to come with me.'

'How will it help?'

'So you can see for yourself what it is like out there.'

We accompanied Chacha in his Land Cruiser. On the way we passed a primary school that had recently been built. A crowd of children were surrounding an object on the football ground.

'What could that be?' I asked.

Chacha drove his vehicle to the school compound. In the midst of the crowd was an old she-elephant lying on the ground. She was too weak to get to her legs. Some children had brought her a bucket of water. She was dipping her trunk laboriously into the bucket for a few sips.

Traditional enemies had become allies in a time of common adversity. We stood in silence while the change of situation began to sink into our minds.

'How do you feel?' Chacha asked softly.

'Sad! Very sad!' Our mood was already beginning to become mellow. That evening the creature died, we were to learn later.

We drove into Masinga. The sight was unbelievable. There were not five or fifteen or fifty elephants of Sher's bygone days. The entire plantation was jam-packed with hungry creatures. There was standing room only inside these seven thousand acres of land. As far as the eye could see there was nothing but dust-covered backs of elephants. Chacha drove his vehicle amidst the crowd. He stopped, took out his rifle and fired repeatedly into the air. Momentarily a few elephants stopped picking at the sisal plants and looked at us. Then they went back to feeding on whatever was left on the ground. Most of them did not give a damn.

This was one of the few occasions when my own eyes were moist. These beasts were dying of hunger and they were eating the only vegetation remaining within their walking distance. Unfortunately, they were eating away *our* sisal. It was an impossible situation. Chacha slowly unloaded his gun.

We drove away from Masinga in silence, never to go there again.

The months of drought rolled on.

As Rustam said, our main concern had to be for the newly planted sisal on the western incline of Voi River. The company had borrowed heavily from the bank for this development. If that section went there would be a financial crisis.

One night Chacha was in a gloomy mood. We were sitting under the tamarind tree outside his house while he made his *tikkis.* Evidently his heart was neither in his cooking nor in his drink.

'I hope this gory business comes to an end some day.' His voice carried sadness. It was understandable. Nobody would like to spend night after night controlling hungry beasts and praying for the nightmare to end.

He remained quiet for a long time, sipping his drink. Then he spoke softly:

'Yesterday evening I went to our new plantation. I reached there in time to see a group of about twenty elephants cross the dry river bed and enter the new sisal block. I fired in the air. The group came to an abrupt halt. They lingered for about five minutes and then started advancing. When they had established themselves inside the field and were about to start plucking small plants I shot one of them down. She fell to the ground, yelling. The rest of the herd took to their heels in a great cloud of dust. In a minute or two they crossed the river and disappeared into bush on the other bank.'

Chacha took a long sip from his glass. From his tone I knew there was something more to come.

'There was this poor baby.' Chacha coughed. 'There was this tiny thing that detached itself from the group of elephants and came running back. I had not realised that the elephant I had shot had a baby. They were all mixed up in a crowd and there were so many females in that group. Anyway, the baby came running to her mother who was lying on the ground. Perhaps it was too young to understand what death meant. It started thumping the mother with its small trunk as if saying, "Get up Mama, this is no time to play the sleeping game. Everyone is gone and we will be left behind. Wake up Mama!" When there was no response from the mother it started circling her, somewhat bewildered. Suddenly it noticed a young sisal plant. It went for it and started chewing it. The creature must have been very hungry.

'A little later the baby came back to its mother and started thumping the dead animal with its trunk. I stood there with my trackers looking at this personification of innocence. I have been a hunter for a long time, but this was one animal I could not lift my gun to. No, not even in the name of mercy. I drove back home when it became too dark to see.'

Chacha's voice was even softer when he spoke again. 'This morning I went to retrieve the tusks from the dead creature. The baby was no longer there. I do not want to even imagine what would have happened to the poor little thing.'

Chacha was tired of doing the job all by himself. He brought in his nephew to assist him. Din was younger, more energetic and quicker with his reflexes. He now started guarding the new plantation. It was no ordinary task to stop the beasts flooding into the area. He scared them away as best he could.

One day Din stopped his vehicle to stretch his legs. He climbed up a small anthill to monitor the situation as he lit his cigarette. It is an unwritten law amongst hunters to keep your gun with you when you are out of your vehicle. He had just taken the first puff when he saw a buffalo charging him from some thirty yards or so. Din's reflexes came to his aid. Before his mind became aware of whatever was happening he was shooting at the buffalo. The creature kept on charging. Din kept on firing. The last bullet was literally fired with the barrel of his rifle inside the animal's mouth. The bullet went through the palate and into the brain. The momentum of the dying animal pushed Din down the anthill.

On return to the camp Din's leg was put in bandages. That buffalo was the last animal to be shot by the company under control work. By mid November there was not a single sisal plant left in the entire Masinga area of the plantation. Neither were there any animals. Living matter of any kind had all perished.

During joint control work by the Game Department with ranchers and farmers, a fairly large number of animals were killed. However, that particular year the majority of them fell victim to merciless hunger and thirst. It would be futile to do guesswork as to how many thousands perished. Wild animals were not the only victims. Cattle carcasses were to be seen in many parts of the lowlands too.

That was the year when even hyenas and vultures were beginning to be lazy. There was too much food around.

'What are we going to do?' I was both depressed and worried. 'How are we going to repay the development loan to our bankers?'

'We will have to cut leaves from old sisal and gradually pay back the bank. They always have been sympathetic towards us. New development is out the question, Rustam summed up the situation.

So for the next seven years we produced sisal fibre from the old plantation which had gradually become overgrown with bush. And we paid back our bankers – shilling by shilling. . . .

Repercussions were to follow. As the years passed by there were whispers about the state of affairs at this particular plantation. The divisional agriculture officer was more blunt: 'You have all that vast track of land which is underproductive.'

What the agriculture officer's textbook did not tell him was what it costs to bulldoze an acre of land, run a ripper through it, plough it, plant young sisal over it and keep the field reasonably weeded for three years before you cut your first sisal leaf. If one happens to be in a semi-arid area, the grower will be lucky to obtain a yield of 300 kilos of fibre per acre per year.

There were forty sisal plantations in the country at one stage. There were hardly twenty that were operational at that time. If we asked to be compensated for the crop destruction from the relevant authority (there is such legal provision), the reply came: 'We are unable to entertain your claim because your farm is mismanaged.' Naturally our farm looked mismanaged. Our plight was no better than that of Chacha's education. Every time he had learnt his alphabet up to letter 'H' he was uprooted from a school. He never made any progress. Every time we planted new sisal plants they were uprooted by elephant during the dry season. We made no progress either.

Not many people were around the day we opened our store and looked in despair at a pile of over a thousand tons of unsold sisal.

Overseas buyers had been coming out with comments like, 'Who needs your natural fibre?' or, 'We have many synthetic materials from which to choose.'

Not many people will remember the night the beekeeper's fire swept over four hundred acres of healthy plants. Thirty miles away the railway station master at Bachuma looked in disbelief at the blazing sky.

Who is there to remember the lean days of the company when the entire mobile transport on the plantation consisted of one Ford tractor? Beginning at eight in the morning and continuing until four in the afternoon old Agwe

Oringo pulled sisal trailers from the field to the factory. After that Rustam would take the tractor to town to purchase our bread, milk, and eggs and then drive home.

Neither will many remember the day the sisal store accidentally burnt down, destroying over a million shillings worth of sisal. The insurance company refuted the claim. They all have their small print.

Nor will many remember when there was not one drop – not one single drop – of rain during an entire ten-month stretch. No, the agriculture officers' textbooks do not give guidelines for such conditions. The words 'marauding elephants' would not be found in the remotest corner of his textbook.

If all these matters have been forgotten then let us, too, conveniently forget those two months when the elephants ran over three thousand acres of sisal plantation.

TWELVE

I was leaning over the wooden railing of the upper verandah late one night. Rustam had gone to sleep earlier on. As had been a long-standing tradition, the small diesel generator supplying electricity to the house had been turned off by the watchman when he had seen the illuminated passenger train snail across the basin far down below. Rustam and I had stayed so long in this house that we had come to take it for granted. Yet the house had its turbulent past.

It was the same house that a zestful Englishman had built some three-quarters of a century back. He had almost reached his El Dorado in this lonely corner of the world, if only a woman had not toppled him down.

It was also the house where both a prince and a pauper had spent some time. The prince was the Prince of Wales, later to become King Edward the Eighth of England. At the time when the prominent British firm owned the plantation the prince was in the vicinity, hunting big game. The local English community had organised a ball in his honour in this house. That was in the early thirties.

The pauper was a man called Tochi. He literally lived and died on a back street of Nairobi. Whenever he ran out of funds for his booze, Chacha used to bring him along, for a moderate fee, as a helper at the hunting camp. If the camp were full, he would come and sleep quietly in the upstairs bedroom of the house. Always smiling; always helpful; always happy. I label him a 'pauper' with some hesitation, but the dictionary fails to offer any other word for a man who is penniless and lives on a street. The world has no time to go on probing the hearts and minds of such flotsam and jetsam of society.

Again, it was in this house where two business partners stayed after accidentally stumbling on a commodity called sisal. In the evenings they smoked incessantly over tea. Then one of them walked into the bathroom one fine morning and closed behind him the door to life itself. Goodness, I thought, as I looked at the plains below, thirty years have passed since that event!

And many more who came to spend their time in the house must have loved and laughed and cried . . . people I do not even know of.

I looked at the clear sky above. It was like being in a planetarium, except this was much bigger in dimension and very real. The sky on that clear, cold night was splashed with millions of stars and planets. Floating amongst the stars was a dazzling white moon which did not seem to be in any particular hurry to sink behind the hills in the west. All the heavenly objects in the sky had turned the landscape below into a soothing silvery hue. I felt small and altogether insignificant under the universe. They say the universe is infinite. In all my life I have not been able to conceive truly what 'infinity' can be. I doubt if there is either a mathematical or logical explanation of the term. And I thought of the Master of all this whom we, for convenience sake, call God. And my futile attempts so far to locate Him – of course, for selfish reasons.

My thoughts turned to the events of that particular day. In the wake of the devastating drought we had no choice but to close down the factory. The area of the plantation that had not been invaded by elephants had dried up so much that the sisal leaves had become hard and tough like leather. Even poor Jarnail Singh could not have been much help then. It was evident that the factory would have to remain closed for a long, long time. Until the rains came; until the new leaves matured; until the workers and machines and ourselves were reorganised.

Late that afternoon the main isolator switch had been thrown down, cutting off life-giving electricity to all the machines. They had obediently stopped throbbing.

We had come home early and sat over tea. There was little to be said, but a lot to be thought. About three-quarters of an hour elapsed before Rustam stated:

'It has got to be developed.'

'What has got to be developed?' I did not have a clue what he was talking about.

'Land,' said Rustam softly. 'We have lost almost everything except land. Where there is land there is hope.'

'You must be joking,' I replied. 'We do not have the funds or the energy to plant new sisal and wait three years for the plants to mature.'

Rustam paused a little before speaking again.

'I was not thinking of sisal. There is this seasonal river along our boundary. Both the floodwater and the subterranean water of this river is flowing down into the Indian Ocean uselessly. Let us trap it. Let us sink shallow wells along the river and grow a small acreage under irrigation. Something, say, liked Capsicum.'

'Or cabbages,' I replied teasing.

'Maybe tomatoes,' said Rustam.

'Or turnips.' I was beginning to find his suggestions positively boring.

We stayed quiet for a long time. Again it was Rustam who broke the silence.

'Land! Land! Land! – there is something strange about land. It remains faithful to one who toils and works on it. Under certain circumstances one can sign a document and disown it. However, the true bond is never broken. That bond is made in heaven.'

I thought my brother was getting a little carried away so I kept quiet.

Now leaning over the railing, I once more looked at the silvery landscape before me. Never, never ending African bushland. The range of hills far out on the right . . . Then suddenly I thought, 'What is so special about it?' In fact, nothing! All the people who spent their time in the house before me must have seen all that I was seeing. More shall see the same sight when I am no longer here. Why feel touched about it. After all, we are all as insignificant as Boris Pasternak's character who, as the great author put it, became 'a nameless number on a list that was afterwards mislaid'.

As the night was becoming chilly I decided to go to sleep. Some time towards morning I dreamt that my father was holding me by my finger and leading me through a row of sisal plants. He was wearing his white topee. I was eleven years old again.

Silly stuff these dreams are . . .

It was a chilly, bleak and windy July afternoon when I first visited Chacha's grave at a cemetery in Nairobi – a heap of soil with wooden planks at each end. Someone had done a poor job in scrawling with oil paint Chacha's full name, together with the dates of his birth and death.

Chacha's death certificate indicated that he had died of 'cardiac arrest'. But that only described the clinical reason for his demise. There was more to it. He had died of heart-break. Not for a woman but for one particular corner of this country and the lifestyle it offered that he had come to love. I can think of a parallel case.

No one could have lived for so long on the doorstep of Tsavo National Park without knowing about the late David Sheldrick. (Or 'Saa Nane' as he was affectionately referred to by his juniors.) He was put in charge of a large area of bushland to convert into a national park. He moved to

Tsavo almost about the same time that we came to Voi. Very painstakingly he cut out roads, graded them, built dams and airstrips, put up signposts. For many years we observed him working tirelessly to convert the bush into one of the most well known national parks: Tsavo National Park, East. After a quarter of a century it was felt that he had grown too senior to be just a park warden. The authorities promoted him to National Park Headquarters in Nairobi. I hope I am not exceeding the realities and the facts if I believe that his mind and body could not accept the new pattern of city life. He died a fairly young person. Sad and premature end of a dedicated soul. He had loved Tsavo as much as anyone can.

Chacha died under similar conditions. When hunting of animals was banned in the country, he had no business hanging around Voi. For a few months the lonely figure was seen sitting under the tamarind tree in his compound. He had no guns, no clients, no tents and no gun bearers. At best we would pay him a call in the evenings. But the glorious days of Signal Hill had melted away. Then he moved to Nairobi. From the window of his flat he saw people and cars madly rushing by. The very last time I met him he pointed his finger to the noisy world outside and asked: 'Look now, where do you think they are all running to?'

I stood for a long time at Chacha's grave. I thought how could a person whose presence could once be felt a mile away, be so quiet now. Just because of what we call 'past'? Suddenly the past revolted and defied my thoughts. It wanted to linger on with those who were still alive. I felt its presence.

Then they began to come. In the beginning their movements were slow and quiet. Then the pace became quicker and they were noisy.

I saw Sher coming as he carefully planted his feet. He had a broad smile on his face. He was flashing his white teeth and rubbing his round cheeks.

Somewhere out of a corner strode Mwagudu, swiftly and softly. He stood by Sher, holding his master's elephant gun.

And Adam came with red, angry eyes, looking very upset.

Suddenly Chacha dashed in like a tornado. He was shouting at the top of his voice.

At a respectable distance stood the Superintendent of Police, Hopkins. He was shaking his head slowly in hopeless dismay.

Then the ground shuddered and an articulated Garrat locomotive, belching thick black cloud of smoke from its chimney, cut through the crowd.

Even the elephants came out of their graves, swaying their trunk gently in the air. They were partly covered in red dust.

All that was dead was alive again... There was a lot of shouting and roaring and thundering. The crescendo had reached an unbearable pitch. I plugged my ears with my fingers and shut my eyes. I began to feel better. When I opened my eyes again they all had faded away to irrevocable past. The only tangible thing remaining was Chacha's silent grave.

As I started walking away I heard distinct ringing of Chacha's voice in my ear.

"Look now, what time has done to me!"

I stopped, turned around and said:

"Chacha, you are not an exception. Time is a cruel monster. It does that to everyone......"

EPILOGUE

BACHUMA STATION. Only when I saw a man in white uniform come out of the station building carrying a 'Hurricane' lamp did I realize that I had lost track of time reminiscing about the past. Our car probably would have been repaired. The sun had long since set and the immediate area was deserted and dark. There was a mild and pleasant wind sweeping from easterly direction. I took one deep breath of pure and fresh air. Despite the thick screen of darkness one could feel the boundlessness and vastness of tranquil African plains. Thirty miles to the west lay Voi, the place about which you had once asked me the question: *"Do you still remember what it was like at Voi in those days?"*

So, that is how and what it was like at Voi in those days as far as I remember.

It would be presumptuous for me to feel that there is something special about all that I have narrated. There is an old tree on the platform of Voi Railway Station, ironically again a baobab tree. On the fat trunk of this tree are scores of names, which would have been carved out many, many years ago, maybe with a penknife or a blade. These are the names of people who at one time or the other were connected with the railway decades back. These names have remained unscathed the by passing of time. Some of the owners of those names have gone away, maybe migrated, but I suspect most of them are dead.

Curiously enough, there is even a name of a woman chipped on one of the rocks around the area. Normally one may assume the job was done by one of her admirers. But the old timers have a different story to tell. It is said that the deep dent was left behind by the young and pretty girl herself as a reminder of times when her own tender feelings were trampled upon, the way our sisal plants were. She was a silent victim of circumstances and reasoning gone mad: of bigotry and home made moral standards. Then she, too, left Africa, never to come back again.

So there were also people with their own private joys and sorrows. All of them must have fairly interesting incidents to remember. I have been fortunate enough to have the luxury of time to recollect those days. Even then, at best, only events can be remembered, but precise feelings cannot be expressed however hard one may try. How does one express what it felt like to breathe the smoke from the trail of a steam locomotive pounding uphill? Or what it was like to sit alone on a lonely hill behind the house on a Sunday afternoon listening to melodious tunes on your transistor radio! Those feelings have to remain buried in the mind of the beholder. No language can unfold them.

Whatever has been narrated about the earlier days of the plantation, I have relied on what the late Mr. Robert ('Bob') Foster had to tell us. Over the number of years I have looked back at shooting of all those elephants during control work with lots of misgivings. It was not pleasant. But it was not unnecessary either.

There was a time when it was difficult to draw a line between human interest and survival of maverick animals. There were more of them than any younger generation can even imagine today. It was not uncommon in those days to hear of a locomotive or a car being hit by one of those wild animals as they roamed freely around the countryside in their hundreds.

On a rare occasion while driving along Mombasa Nairobi road I see the setting sun screened off by clouds, creating an amber glow. I stop the vehicle. Soft thoughts float by of those days and of them who have disappeared in the ever-darkening shadow of time. I think of Sheriff who thought that life was an unending joke, or of Vithal who could not understand why he was constantly surrounded by hostilities. Sher was one person who gave all he had to try to fool all the people all the time, and almost succeeded. No one can come near enough to Mwagudu if standard of loyalty is ever questioned. Perhaps Adam was the evil that Nature sent to keep the balance between good and bad. Chacha roared and thundered and enjoyed his whisky......and life. Poor Assistant Superintendent of Police, Hopkins, was caught up in this circus in the course of his somewhat unpleasant duty. There was bad and good in all of them. But on balance they made a great and memorable crowd. To the world at large they are all dead and gone. But I remember them. Very vividly!

Some three miles down the road from Voi to Mombasa there is a tall steel tower on the left. It forms part of booster station for Voice of Kenya. That tower and beyond was the Masinga section of the farm. That is where animals and we were locked in the struggle for territorial rights. In the end they lost their lives and we lost all our sisal.

I have never been there again but am told that when the rains are gone, and cooler months of June and July set in, the place is carpeted with creepers with an abundance of flowers. It may be coincidental but the colour of the flower is white.

In those days there was graffiti on a large boulder by the bush track as one drove out of Masinga to join the pipeline road on way to Voi. Some lone soul, for reasons that could only be of personal nature, had scrawled:

The taste of wine
Is not forgotten...
Though the vessel be
No more......

Coast Province, Kenya
12th December 1986